CW00641332

WHAT GOD HAS *NOT* UNITED

Paul Robbins

MINERVA PRESS
ATLANTA LONDON SYDNEY

WHAT GOD HAS *NOT* UNITED
Copyright © Paul Robbins 1996

All Rights Reserved

ISBN 1 85863 940 9

First Published 1996 by
MINERVA PRESS
Sixth Floor
Canberra House
315–317 Regent Street
London W1R 7YB

2nd Impression 1997
3rd Impression 1997
4th Impression 1998

Printed in Great Britain for Minerva Press

WHAT GOD HAS *NOT* UNITED

To my parents

Acknowledgements

I wish to thank all those who have assisted me in the writing of this book, either in their encouragement of this venture or in their practical assistance. In particular, I wish to express my thanks to my parents Tess and John Robbins, Mrs Sheila O'Neill and Fathers Roger Daley and Peter Wilkinson for reading the text at an early stage and offering me their thoughts and suggestions; Mrs Maureen McKenna for her valuable and practical insights which assisted in making the text more comprehensible; and Father Francis Morrisey OMI for his observations and suggestions in the final stages of writing. I also wish to express my gratitude to the Canon Law Society of Great Britain and Ireland for permission to quote various canons from *The Code of Canon Law in English Translation* (1983).

Preface

When two people exchange consent in a ceremony of marriage, they do not always succeed in entering the married state.

"Are you ready, freely and without reservation, to give yourselves to each other in marriage?" is the first question put to them in the wedding ceremony. It expresses the nature of Christian marriage as a mutual gift of one person to another. When each of the bride and groom says "I am", they are affirming that it is their intention to form a permanent partnership of life with each other which is for their mutual benefit and, if it is God's will, for the procreation and education of children. Such is the ideal of marriage.

Yet many marriages do not work. This book takes as its subject those marriages that fail to be permanent, and examines how the Catholic Church determines whether or not they were truly marriages.

Reactions to the contents of this book might vary from surprise and bewilderment for some to hope and optimism for others. To some, it might seem like an attack on all that the Church teaches regarding the sacrament of marriage. To others, particularly those who have suffered marriage breakdown and who may even have entered a second union, it may bring some comfort and even open the way to closer union with God and the Church.

There is nothing contained in these pages which contradicts the teachings and discipline of the Catholic Church. Indeed, I would suggest that the practices which are outlined here actually strengthen the Church's teaching that marriage is a partnership of conjugal life and love which has as its ends the well-being of the couple and the procreation and education of children [Vatican II, *Gaudium et spes*, n.48]. For it is certain that many marriages fall far short of this, and Church teaching can lack conviction if it does not appear to reflect reality. Hence, that the Church has the facility to declare null and void a marriage which never succeeded in becoming a "partnership of conjugal life and love" lends credibility to its teaching, and its desire to portray what is inherent in human nature, that marriage is a good and desirable institution.

Despite the fact that some 40% of marriages are now failing, the Church will and must always continue to stress the sacramentality of marriage, the fundamental expression of which is its permanence. That is a teaching from Christ himself, and thus is not open to dissension. The Church must also continue to do all within its power to ensure that couples are given every opportunity to make their marriages work. This should begin, for the couple at least, as soon as marriage is contemplated. For a decision with such consequences – to make a gift of oneself to one other person for as long as both are alive – it is important that the couple both understand the nature of marriage and have a relationship which will sustain the promises made on the wedding day. Marriage preparation is most important, and probably even more so today when society, so influenced by the media, presents the marriage promises as easily put aside.

Within marriage, too, the Church can assist by providing support for newly married couples, giving them an ear to talk through the difficulties they are facing and their worries and fears. There is no substitute for the spouses themselves being open about their difficulties and being willing to tackle them together, but there is no doubt that the intervention of a third party, such as a marriage guidance counsellor, is sometimes beneficial. If difficulties are not faced or the couple are unable to make their partnership work in all areas of life, there will inevitably be an increased vulnerability to marriage breakdown.

In all broken marriages, one of the parties would have reached a crisis point beyond which it was impossible to remain with the other in an attempt to make their marriage work. Until that point is reached, there might well be a chance that the marriage could be saved. As long as there remains some hope of success, the couple themselves and the Church as a whole have a duty to uphold the sacrament of marriage by encouraging the couple to remain faithful to the promises made on the wedding day.

That having been said, the starting point for this book is marriage breakdown, for whatever reason. What then do the parties have to look forward to within the Church? Are they condemned to a life separated or divorced from the spouse, yet bound by the promises made on the wedding day? What if they meet other people with whom they fall in love and eventually desire to marry? Is a second marriage possible without abandoning the faith or the sacraments? What is contained in these pages will, I hope, lead the reader to find an answer to some of these questions.

Contents

Section I

Chapter One

The Church and Marriage Breakdown

Perhaps the greatest threat to the faith of a believer is a reluctance to let that faith develop. Faith is not something which is static. Faith is a journey of discovery; a journey in which, if we are properly disposed, the Holy Spirit will lead us continually to a greater awareness of the truth of God's love for us.

We find God in many ways, not the least of which is through one another and the experiences of everyday life. This means that faith is constantly challenged. The barrage of new experiences in life means that, from time to time, the believer will be confronted with a situation which suggests that his faith is wrong. Common sense will tell him one thing and his faith another. For the sake of peace of mind, one must give way. After all, there is surely nothing in this world which cannot be reconciled with the God who made this world. The believer must come to accept that his understanding of truth is flawed, and he is challenged to seek a new understanding as part of his journey of faith.

In recent years, one of the greatest challenges to the faith of individual members of the Catholic Church has resulted from the number of marriages which have failed. The Church teaches that marriage is a permanent institution, yet the divorce rate continues to rise, and people remarry seemingly as though they have never made marriage promises before. The Church teaches that full sexual relations are proper only between husband and wife, but the media present us with soap operas and other fictional works which disregard the concept of fidelity, and surveys which would confirm the fiction as fact. The Church teaches that marriage is for the good of the couple and the procreation and education of children, and yet the pressures of modern society are to put self before others, and success (often measured in monetary terms) before salvation.

These conflicting messages can be a challenge to believers. Yet, an even greater challenge can occur if they experience marriage breakdown themselves or see someone they love battling with that pain. At such times, religious values can seem to do nothing but add to the pain. Catholics and others, who have all their lives upheld the belief that marriage is for life, may find the pain of marriage breakdown greater than those who do not accept such beliefs. This can be made worse if there is an absence of support from the Church community. In such circumstances, there is a danger that feelings of guilt and a sense of failure will cause irreparable spiritual damage.

For anyone who believes that marriage is for life, and this is particularly true for those whose Churches so often affirm the permanent nature of marriage, the breakdown of their own marriage can seem like an alienation from God. Many choose to remain simply separated from their spouses rather than seek a divorce. Some believe that, by doing this, they are being faithful to a biblical teaching that divorce is not acceptable (*Mark* 10:1-12). When the former spouse forces a divorce on them through the courts, they console themselves with the knowledge that it was not of their own making.

Others, however, find that legal separation is not enough and so seek divorce themselves. For those who see divorce as contrary to the teachings of Jesus, it is worthwhile reflecting on His teaching in its context. Jesus says:

> . . .what God has united man must not divide. [. . .]
> The man who divorces his wife and marries another is
> guilty of adultery against her, and if a woman divorces
> her husband and marries another, she is guilty too.
> (*Mark* 10:9,11-12)

Jesus, then, talks of divorce as the dividing of something which God has united. When remarriage follows the division of this God-made union, there is the guilt of adultery.

What is significant about this statement of Jesus is that it is in the context of remarriage that He focuses on divorce. This is also true of His statement on divorce in the gospel of Saint Luke (16:18). It is in this context of remarriage that He refers to divorce as sin. He does not say that divorce is a sin in the situation of a marital union becoming an intolerable burden for one spouse to the extent that separation and divorce are the only feasible options.

But perhaps of greater significance is that Jesus talks of marriage in its spiritual aspect; something God has made. He does not see marriage simply in terms of two people agreeing to form a community of life together. He sees it as a part of God's plan. He talks of something God has united. It flows from this that the bond is permanent. God has created that bond and so no one can divide it. This creates a difficulty when it comes to the permanence of individual marriages, for who is to say that God has or has not united two people in marriage?

The Church does not try to provide a universal answer to this question; it presumes that those who take part in a marriage ceremony have been united by God in marriage. As far as the Catholic Church is concerned, all marriages are considered true marriages until such time as it might be shown otherwise. The result of this is that all marriages must be considered as lasting for life.

The Church presumes that God unites all who exchange consent, and therefore it is not possible for a person to remarry while the spouse is still alive. Yet, who can know the mind of God? As will be shown later, it can be said with certainty that not everyone who exchanges consent to marriage actually succeeds in entering the married state. To put it another way, God does not unite two people just because they perform a wedding ceremony. Not every wedding produces a marriage. Consequently, should these people later separate or divorce, they cannot always be said to be dividing that which God has united. It is impossible to estimate the proportion of marriage failures which involve couples whom God has not united, but if diocesan statistics of successful applications for declarations of nullity are a reliable guide, the proportion is much higher than most people would imagine.

This possibility, that not all married couples have been united by God, means that those who talk of divorce in the Church must choose their words carefully. It is in the context of the division of a God-made union for the purpose of remarriage that Jesus talks of divorce as wrong. If all divorce is condemned as wrong or evil, there is a danger of making false judgments and heaping guilt on to the consciences of people already suffering the pain of marriage breakdown. Divorce is often the only realistic option after a failed marriage, and Jesus does not appear to condemn divorce in such circumstances.

The danger of condemning divorcees can also be seen from a more simple and logical approach, although it still finds its source in that same teaching of Jesus. But first it is important to understand the distinction between civil law and Church law, which is called canon law (the individual laws are referred to as "canons" and the "Code of canon law" is the collection of canons).

Civil law deals with the rights and duties of individuals living within a certain geographical area – for example, England or Scotland. Canon law deals with the rights and duties of individuals of common faith – in this book, members of the Roman Catholic Church. Thus, Catholics living in England are subject both to English civil law and the canon law of the Roman Catholic Church. They may also be subject to the laws of another country if they are a national of that country, just as English nationals do not escape English law simply by going abroad.

In the context of marriage, a Catholic marrying in England must fulfil both the provisions of civil law and of canon law. For this reason, not only must a Catholic marriage be witnessed by a priest or deacon, but a civil registrar must also be present. Sometimes the priest might also be a civil registrar, in which case he simultaneously performs duties both for the Church and for the State.

On the subject of marriage separation, canon law recognises certain situations in which one party can lawfully leave the other. Whilst certain cases of adultery are specifically mentioned in the Code of canon law, separation is recognised as a realistic option when there might be grave danger to the soul or body of children of the couple or to one of the spouses if they stay together. Indeed, the Code goes so far as to say that separation is possible in circumstances in which living together becomes too difficult. Thus, the Church recognises that situations will arise in which the separation of a married couple is fully justifiable.

On the subject of divorce, however, canon law has nothing to say. Divorce does not exist in canon law, and divorce from a Catholic marriage does not exist in reality. If, then, divorce from a Catholic marriage does not exist, it is nonsense even to talk of the divorce of a Catholic marriage, let alone refer to it as wrong or evil.

When a Catholic refers to himself or herself as being divorced, he or she is talking of a divorce granted in civil law. Hence, a Catholic who obtains a divorce through the civil courts is still recognised as being married according to canon law, although not according to civil law. A civil law divorce can have only civil law effects, and it is for those civil law effects – such as distribution of assets, custody of children – that many seek divorce. The Church's stance on divorce is in opposition to the implied inherent right to remarry which divorce carries, rather than against a divorce which puts an end to a dangerous or impossible situation.

Failure to understand the important distinction between civil and canon law has led in the past to grave injustices in the Church, and not just through careless use of such phrases as "the evil of divorce". In the past, divorced Catholics have been mistakenly forbidden from holding certain offices, judged as sinners by clergy and laity alike, and even barred from the Eucharist.

Civil law divorce, in itself, has no effect on a person's status within the Church. It only affects his or her status in civil law. Hence, whereas the Church should always do its utmost to avoid the breakdown of marriage, it cannot assume that those who are divorced are greater sinners than anyone else. It cannot be stressed enough, therefore, that a person who has obtained a civil law divorce should normally continue to enjoy all the privileges of membership of the Church as though the civil law marriage continued in existence. It is when a divorced person seeks to remarry that difficulties may arise.

Like many of the tragedies of life, it is certainly difficult to appreciate the trauma of marriage breakdown without actually suffering it. Some compare it to bereavement in that, when the marriage fails, a part of the self also dies. Whatever was the state of the relationship, the breakdown is still the final shattering of hopes and dreams and perhaps an admission of failure. It represents the transition from one way of life to a completely different one. It is important to realise that marriage breakdown for a believer will not have occurred without much soul-searching, and divorce will have been a last resort. For a believer, such decisions are not made without prayer, thought and openness to God through conscience. Divorce is never an easy option and those in the Church who condemn divorce risk pronouncing judgment on people to whom they should be offering support.

There is little doubt that, because of the ease with which civil law allows divorce, a few people are moving from one relationship to another without any real thought of the cost to their partners or society as a whole. Such selfishness is contrary to the gospel and would be one of the practices which the Church seeks to condemn in its criticism of divorce. Pronouncements against divorce are also made to discourage anyone from entering marriage lightly and to encourage those experiencing marriage difficulties to use every means at their disposal to reconcile their differences. Seen in this light, the Church's condemnation of divorce is not an attack on individual divorcees, but an attempt by the Church to promote the teaching of Jesus that marriage is for life.

The reality is, however, that some marriages cannot be saved. When a marriage does fail, the parties can feel that the only way they can remain loyal to the teachings of the Church is to spend the rest of their lives without the partnership and companionship they were looking for when they entered marriage. This causes real conflict if they meet someone with whom they would wish to enter marriage.

The remaining chapters will explain how remarriage can be possible for some people by obtaining a declaration that the first union was not a valid marriage. There is also a section which explains how a declaration of nullity is obtained in practice. The final section of the book examines the Church's approach to some particular situations of marriage breakdown and its approach to those in second unions who are unable to obtain a declaration of nullity.

Marriage annulment (to use the more common term), however, cannot realistically be understood without an understanding of marriage. A brief summary of the Church's teaching on and understanding of marriage is the subject of the next chapter.

Chapter Two

Are You Ready, Freely And Without Reservation...?

The Church teaches the important role marriage plays in family life and society in general. In the face of so many marriages breaking down, Church teaching also constantly emphasises the permanent nature of marriage. After all, if a marriage is God-made, the couple are walking their path to salvation, and the Church is doing nothing more than urging the couple to be faithful to God's call to them.

In the documents of the Second Vatican Council, the idea of marriage as covenant was expressed. The word "covenant" is used in the Old Testament to describe the relationship between God and His chosen people. It was expressed in the phrase "You will be my people and I will be your God" (cf. *Jeremiah* 7:23). There was an understanding between God and His people that He would watch over them provided they kept His laws. With the coming of Jesus, a new covenant is formed which is linked to the old. Jesus, by His death on the cross, becomes the mediator between God and His people. God so loved the world that He sent His only son. Now, in the new covenant, believers are asked by God to "love one another as I have loved you" (*John* 13:34).

This new covenant is the example of love to be copied by married couples. Jesus gave his life for the Church and this is the supreme example of how Christians should approach marriage: the giving of one's life to another person for his or her good.

This teaching of the Church is beautifully expressed in Pope Paul VI's Encyclical, *Humanae Vitae*. He sets the marital union in the context of God's plan for mankind. It is, he says, the realization of "His design of love" (*Humanae Vitae*, n.8).

Pope Paul VI describes the gift of husband and wife to one another as "the reciprocal personal gift of self". Herein lies the essence of the marital relationship and that which distinguishes it from all other relationships. The marital relationship is unique in that it constitutes the unreserved gift of one person to another, and the acceptance of that gift by the other, for the well-being of each and, if God wills, the forming of new life in children.

Nevertheless, the reality would appear to be that many married people have failed to grasp this fundamental element of the marriage covenant, and this despite the fact that the first question to which they respond in the marriage ceremony is: "are you ready, freely and *without reservation*, to give yourselves to each other in marriage?"

The nature of this relationship sets marriage apart from the so-called live-in arrangement (which the Church would in any case consider unacceptable) when a couple decide to live together rather than marry. They may share the same roof over their heads, a car, a bed and meals. They may share some finances and even be parents of the same child(ren). Yet, unless they have made that gift of self to the other, and expressed that in the giving of consent, they have not entered the state of matrimony.

An interesting historical note emerges here. A so-called common law marriage arises when a couple live together holding themselves out to be man and wife when in fact they have never taken part in a public ceremony of marriage, or otherwise formally exchanged consent. The idea of consent by implication can arise and certain rights can attach in law. In canon law, for example, the impediment of public propriety arises when a couple live together in what the law calls "a notorious or public concubinage" [canon 1093], which could correspond to a common law marriage. The result is that a party to such a union may not later marry a descendant or ancestor of the other.

For example, if Alfonzo and Beatrice live together for a number of years in such a way that it is common knowledge that they are enjoying all the benefits of marriage without actually being married, Alfonzo cannot later marry Beatrice's widowed mother even though both might technically be free. Similarly, if Alfonzo had a son from a previous relationship, the son and Beatrice would be considered ineligible to marry one another.

Despite these common law arrangements being termed marriages, the lack of a formal exchange of consent means that they can never properly be recognised in law as true marriages. They also differ from the live-in arrangement in that the couple will, in some way, hold themselves out as being married, whereas those who live-in have often quite deliberately rejected the idea of marriage for at least the immediate future.

The essence of the gift of self which is marriage is further expressed in the marriage ceremony when the parties call upon those present to witness that each takes the other "to have and to hold from this day forward, for better for worse, for richer for poorer, in sickness and in health, to love and to cherish, till death do us part". In other words, no matter what happens to me or to you in the future, we will remain united in marriage until the death of one of us.

This is the permanent aspect of marriage. The gift of self in marriage is a gift without reservation. Consequently, it can only be such a gift if it lasts until the death of one of the parties. From time to time, it is suggested that the problems of marriage breakdown might be eased if marriages could be temporary. Whatever such a temporary union might be called, it is not a marriage because it does not involve the unreserved gift of self.

This permanent aspect of marriage is both awesome and wonderful. It is awesome in its implications of exclusivity (forsaking all others), and yet wonderful in the elements of trust, friendship and respect which can develop.

In the ideal marriage, the couple make a true gift of self to one another and succeed in establishing a partnership of life which is mutually beneficial. It can be said of such marriages that the trials and tribulations of everyday life are not found within the marital relationship, but are a burden shared by the couple as one. Most married couples would admit, however, that the process of two becoming one is lifelong, and many would probably admit that their marriage was not ideal because of differences in character and personality which they had not succeeded in bridging and which they could never envisage being satisfactorily overcome. They would see these differences as a lack of perfection in their marriage rather than a potential cause of breakdown. Consequently, there are probably very few couples who would claim to have an ideal marriage, although some realists might contend that their marriage could not have been more happy, and in that sense was ideal.

The process of two becoming one is the on-going task of marriage. Those who fail to realise that, who perhaps give up trying after the wedding day, have failed to understand that gift of self. The taking of the other expressed on the wedding day is possible only if the other makes that gift of self; and the essence of marriage is the day-to-day give and take – the "reciprocal personal gift of self", as I put it in Chapter VI called it. The essence of marriage is found in the daily manifestation of selfless giving to the other. That is the covenant: the ceaseless attempting to enhance the good of the other, whilst also receiving that gift from the other. Unless that desire to make a gift of self to the other underlies the decision to marry, the potential for future marriage failure must be present.

Chapter Three
Marriage and Vocation

So far, I have tried to explain something of the nature of marriage and to link this with the statement of Jesus that man must not divide what God has united. Marriage nullity, on a practical level, appears to contradict this teaching of Jesus regarding the permanence of marriage. If a marriage is declared invalid, it is almost always after the couple have lived together as husband and wife for a period of time. In fact, what a declaration of nullity is saying is that one or both of the marriage partners did not, for one reason or another, make that necessary gift of self to the other. Although it is sometimes possible to recognise before the wedding that a certain proposed marriage has little chance of succeeding, it is usually only after the couple have attempted to live out their married life that the truth emerges.

The marriage nullity process seeks to discover if the essence of a particular marriage was missing. For, if the essence was missing, it cannot have been a marriage. If it was not a marriage, it was not one of the "God-united" unions to which Jesus refers. It is surely right, then, that believing couples wishing to marry should attempt to discern if their decision accords with the will of God, both for their happiness in this life and, because marriage is a sacrament, for their ultimate salvation.

The Church, too, can only gain by helping couples to make wise and prayerful decisions in their choice of lifelong partners. The Church exists ultimately for the salvation of its members. If one couple suffers by entering a marriage which ultimately breaks down, the Church as a whole suffers. Consequently, it is important for the Church as a whole to do whatever it can to assist couples to examine their decision to marry, and for the couple themselves to be properly disposed to examining and being honest about the state of their relationship, their motives for marriage and the appropriateness of their choice of lifelong partner.

How can a couple be sure that what they are doing is God's will; in other words, that what they are doing is entering a God-made union? The truth is we can never know for sure that any action is in accord with the will of God. We can only attempt to discern the proposed course of action over a period of time and then, if things seem to be right, take a leap in faith. There are certain guidelines which can help in that discernment, but they can never prevent mistakes being made.

In several places in the gospels can be found the idea that God knows each one of us intimately. In the gospel of St Matthew (6:6), we are told that God sees all that is done in secret. In the gospel of St Luke (12:7), we find the statement that every hair on your head is known to God. In the gospel of St John (1:45,47–49) is the story of Nathanael meeting Jesus for the first time and being greeted by Jesus saying of him: "there is an Israelite who deserves the name *incapable of deceit*", thus indicating that Jesus already knows Nathanael intimately.

If we can accept that God knows each of us in this way, we can begin to realise that each of us is unique in His eyes and that each of us has a part to play in His plan for mankind. Our spiritual relationship with Him will necessarily be based on the recognition that we are playing some small, and not necessarily revealed, part in His plan. We will seek to find out what that part is, but it will be a lifelong search. Even those who have seemingly found their vocation can only admit that they have taken one step forward. The man who decides he is called to the priesthood has only begun his journey of discovery of his vocation, because his call does not stop there. He must decide if he is called to the contemplative life or to a ministry requiring more interaction with the laity. He must then decide if he is called to join a Religious Order or a diocese, and which one. Since priests are now given a much greater say in the type of work they undertake, he may later have to decide if his ministry is to be in hospitals, a parish, with youth, teaching or elsewhere. His call may later require even greater service in the role of bishop, cardinal or even pope.

Likewise, the call to marriage is only one step of a journey: a journey which requires a continuous and lifelong attempt to enhance the life of the spouse, in such a way that it gives the other complete freedom to grow and to reciprocate for the good of both. Together they can discover if they are called to be parents, of one or perhaps more children, and in what way their marriage can add value to the wider community outside the immediate family.

It can be seen from this that, if we are to discover the fullness of the call that God makes to each of us, there must be a continuing relationship with Him.

How can we know that God is calling us to one particular vocation rather than another? The answer to this is within ourselves. God's call for each of us is a fundamental part of who we are. What He wants each of us to be is found within the individual person He created. As we grow in knowledge of ourselves, as we learn about our strengths and weaknesses, each of us gradually comes to a limited awareness of what it is and what it is not possible for us to do with our lives, and particularly what we want to do with our lives.

It is these particular desires, the deepest desires of my being, that are the best guide to God's call for me. The idea that God, who is love, would call any of us to a life of unhappiness is unthinkable. His call for each of us is that which will give us total fulfilment, even if we might only reach that point at the end of time.

This can be explained in another way using an example found in the Scriptures. One of the purposes for which God created fig trees is to produce figs, and we might say that an element of the vocation of a fig tree, even the primary element, is the production of figs. Hence, if a fig tree was failing to produce figs, it can be said to be failing to do that for which it was created. This is the point which Jesus was making in the parable of the barren fig tree (cf. *Luke* 13:6–9), and when one day he looked for figs on a tree and found only leaves, he responded in such a way that the tree withered (*Matthew* 21:18–19).

We are all called to some vocation, but its nature is not always clear. There are various ways in which we can seek to discover the nature of that vocation, but a study of the methods of prayerful decision-making is beyond the scope of this book, and the reader should look elsewhere. Nevertheless, there are some more obvious points which can be made here. The starting point in finding God's call has to be from within the person each of us is now. What we were a year ago, or even yesterday, is irrelevant except insofar as it determines who each of us is now. God will never call me to be something which is impossible, and yet what is possible for God should never be underestimated.

Since God calls each of us from within ourselves, we cannot hope to be able to recognise that call without some sort of realistic grasp of who we are. An extreme example of a lack of realism would be the case of a man who claimed he had a vocation to be a mother. However, even though that seems ridiculous, it should not necessarily be ignored out of hand. The man can clearly not be a mother, but it may only be his interpretation of his calling that is wrong. Hopefully, with good guidance and prayer, he could be brought to a more realistic interpretation of the feelings or desires which led him to conclude that he was called to motherhood.

In determining my own vocation, feelings are very important. Again, there is the danger of over-simplifying a complex issue, and only some basic principles can be mentioned here. Broadly speaking, an action which is compatible with the essence of my being will lead to a feeling of contentment, a deep-felt awareness that it is right, and an inner peace. Likewise, an action which is incompatible with my being will leave an uncomfortable feeling; perhaps a pang of conscience; a feeling of "this is not me"; an awareness that something is wrong; general anxiety. These are not the momentary feelings of happiness, sadness, joy, pain, frustration or any of the thousand different feelings we experience naturally every day. It might be exciting to steal a bar of chocolate and a joy to consume it, but my deep-seated knowledge is that I have done wrong (cf. *Proverbs* 20:17).

The person who is living a life in accordance with God's will, that is according to his or her vocation, will experience over time an air of peace and contentment from within, no matter what trials and tribulations might come in everyday life (cf. the warning contained in the reward for those who follow Jesus – *Mark* 10:28–31). Likewise, the person who is trying to live a life which is not in accordance with the will of God will experience over time a deep-seated anxiety or disturbance. It is often said of those who are wicked: "I don't know how they live with themselves." This is precisely the point which is being made.

In the gospel of St Luke (7:36–50), we are told of the woman who, when Jesus was at table, came in and wept over his feet, wiping them with her hair and anointing them with ointment. Jesus refers to her great love because of her knowledge of the forgiveness of her sins. He then says to her: "Your faith has saved you; go in peace." By telling her to "go in peace", Jesus is merely acknowledging the peace of mind the woman feels at the knowledge that she is again at one with God; a peace which would have been absent from her earlier sinful life.

Later, in the same gospel, the story of Zacchaeus is found (19:1-10). He was one of the senior tax collectors and a wealthy man. Tax collectors were empowered by the authorities to collect taxes. It is said that they were not paid for this work, and were allowed instead to remunerate themselves by collecting too much tax and keeping the surplus. Because they had authority to collect tax, nobody could stop them taking too much, and it was easy for them to become very rich. Merely to be a tax collector automatically branded you a sinner. Zacchaeus recognised that he was as guilty of that as anyone, and his immediate response to his life being touched by God was to promise to give half his property to the poor and to repay four times anyone he had cheated. To this, Jesus responds: "Today salvation has come to this house."

In both the story of the woman who used her hair to wipe the feet of Jesus and the story of Zacchaeus, we can see two people who recognised that their lives were in need of change. It would seem that this openness to change is an essential condition for the discovery of God's will in its fullness. It would be wrong ever to presume that the fullness of God's call has been reached.

These aids to finding God's will are as applicable to marriage as any other vocation. When Jesus referred to that which God has united, he implied that the couple were responding to God's call. In an ideal world, this would be true of all marriages. In reality, however, people marry for many different reasons, only some of which can be said to be a response to God's call.

Those who refer to the decision to marry as "it felt right", or "we loved one another in a way that we had never experienced before, and which did not seem to diminish", or "we couldn't imagine living the rest of our lives without one another", might be said to have been responding to a call from God. Those who appeared to marry only because she was pregnant by him, because she liked the size of his bank balance, because they enjoyed a good physical relationship or because it gave each the opportunity to get away from home, might still have responded to God's call (His ways must never be underestimated), but might also be entering a union which was never any part of God's plan. The implications of these motives for marriage nullity will hopefully become more obvious later.

It is important to avoid the idea that in happy marriages the couple have been united by God, and in unhappy marriages they have not. Individual free will and the possibility of sin can render a true marriage unhappy. Equally, two married people might quite happily live their own lives without ever making that gift of self to the other which would render their union a true marriage. Because they are quite happy living their own lives, their so-called marriage can survive.

The first question in the marriage ceremony is: "Are you ready, freely and without reservation, to give yourselves to each other in marriage?" As has been explained already, this gift of self is a part of the very essence of marriage. A gift of myself without reservation must necessarily mean two things. A gift of myself to one person necessarily excludes all other people. I cannot make an unreserved gift of myself to one person in marriage if I am also going to give to another in a manner which detracts from that first gift. Similarly, an unreserved gift implies a permanent gift. A temporary gift is not a gift without reservation.

Another way of saying this is that permanence is part of the very nature of marriage; that is, it flows from the very nature of the desire to make an unreserved gift of self. If this is true, and I do not think that it can be seriously challenged, it is a most serious matter for a true marriage to break down. For, what has happened in marriage breakdown (and this is referring only to true marriages, by which is meant marriages in which that unreserved gift has been made by both partners) is that the marriage has taken a course which is against its own nature. Hence, for a true marriage to break down, it must have happened that one or both of the parties took some action which amounted to a withdrawal of that gift of self made on the wedding day. If that has not happened, and the marriage has broken down, the possibility that it was never a true marriage must be considered.

From all that has been said in this chapter, there would appear to be sound arguments for letting people make their own decisions about the validity or otherwise of their marriage. If one or both parties can honestly say with hindsight that their marriage was never a God-made union, they should be declared free to enter another union.

Unfortunately, this is all very well in theory, but in practice it would simply be unworkable. For one thing, people find it very difficult to be objective about their own circumstances. Many excuses could be found for declaring a broken marriage to be a union which was not God-made. Conversely, it can happen that people who have suffered the most horrendous marriage remain convinced that it nevertheless was a marriage "because that was the promise I made to God". It sometimes seems to be forgotten that it takes two people to make a gift of self for a marriage to work.

Another reason for preventing people from making their own decisions about God's action or lack of it in their coming together is that not everyone would be honest enough to examine their broken marriage from the spiritual aspect. There would be a temptation to abuse such freedom and move from marriage to marriage. Such abuse would make a mockery of Jesus' teaching on the permanence of marriage.

For very obvious reasons, then, marriages are strictly controlled by rules and regulations. A study of the Church's approach to the law which underlies marriage is helpful to an understanding of declarations of nullity of marriage, and is the subject of the next chapter.

Chapter Four

Marriage and the Law of the Church

It has already been noted that the Church presumes that all who exchange consent in a ceremony of marriage are considered to have entered the married state. Besides the need to protect the sanctity of marriage, this presumption seeks to prevent the chaos that could occur if people were party to a wedding ceremony but then, for whatever reason, declared themselves to be unmarried.

In practice, this can be quite difficult to prevent. An attempt is made to prevent people entering a second marriage by asking the parties to declare before the exchange of consent that there is no impediment (see Chapter 7) to their entering marriage. Another attempt is made in English law to prevent bigamous marriages by asking those present if they know of any reason why the couple cannot be joined in marriage. It is hoped that, if anyone is present who is aware that the bride or groom is attempting to marry again, that person would have the courage to make a statement of the fact.

In the Catholic Church, a third safeguard is introduced. A person becomes a Catholic by being baptised into the Church or, if already baptised but not a Catholic, by a formal act of reception. At that time, a record will be made in a register at the place of baptism or reception. Before performing a marriage ceremony, the priest will request each Catholic who is a party to the wedding to obtain a recent baptismal certificate. When a priest performs a wedding ceremony, he must inform the parish priest of the place where the baptism or reception is registered. That parish priest, for his part, is bound to enter the fact of that marriage in the baptismal register. In this way, when a recent baptismal certificate is issued, it will not only give details of the baptism or reception, but also of any previous marriage.

However, even this is not foolproof. Registers can be lost or destroyed; for example, at a time of war. People can forget where they were baptised or simply never have known; if, for example, they were parted from their parents or other relatives before they were old enough to find out where they were baptised. Sometimes, for many different reasons, there is a failure to keep proper records. These difficulties would not prevent the marriage taking place. They would merely take away one of the safeguards against a person entering a bigamous union.

The Church has written many laws to safeguard the sacrament of marriage, and the presumption that all those who are party to a wedding ceremony enter the married state has been embodied in canon law. Of the 1,752 canons of the 1983 Code of canon law, no less than 148 deal specifically with marriage. The principal areas with which the canons deal are: the nature of marriage and the effects of marriage; those who can and cannot enter marriage; the procedures for entering marriage, and who may preside at a wedding ceremony; when and how the bond of marriage can be dissolved, and separation without dissolution. They also deal with how marriages can be declared invalid, and how invalid marriages can be convalidated.

In all that follows in the next few chapters, one assumption will be made throughout. It is an assumption which is embodied in canon law in the presumption that all marriages are valid, and it forms the basis upon which the Church approaches individual marriages and the actions of married people. This assumption is that the legal status of a marriage reflects the truth of that marriage. It is an assumption which is necessary to allow the Church to maintain some sort of order over the ability of the faithful to enter marriage, and so to apply the teaching of Jesus that marriages are permanent. Nevertheless, the possibility of nullity, in which the legal status of a marriage is changed to reflect the reality that a marriage does not exist, is one recognition that sometimes this assumption is incorrect.

A marriage is valid if all the essential conditions for bringing it into existence are fulfilled. If the marriage is valid, the couple become husband and wife. If an essential condition is not met, the marriage is invalid. As will become clear in later chapters, it might not be known for several years, or it may never be known, that an essential condition has not been met. To avoid any undue speculation, embarrassment or other unpleasantness that could arise from any doubt about the validity of a marriage, the Church presumes that all marriages are valid, unless the contrary is proved. Thus, even if it becomes certain that an essential condition was not met, validity continues to be presumed. This presumption only ceases if a declaration of nullity or a decree of dissolution is issued.

There is, then, an important distinction to be made between validity and legality. Validity is concerned with the essence of an action or state. Legality is concerned with its status in law. Thus, marriages are lawful if they are celebrated according to the norms of law. The law also presumes that they are valid; that is, that the marriage has actually come into existence. Note that validity is only presumed. While all possible steps are taken to ensure that a marriage is actually valid, there is no process for declaring it as such.

Consider the following example which, although unlikely, nevertheless might help with an understanding of the difference between legality and validity:

> John and Karen celebrate their wedding. From the moment they exchange consent they are legally married and presumed by law to be validly married. John, however, having lost his memory in an accident before meeting Karen, has forgotten that he is already married. Consequently, his marriage to Karen is invalid, but still legal and even presumed valid. It does not exist in reality, but it does exist in law. He is legally married to two wives, but only validly married to the first. Should the true situation be revealed, steps would be taken to correct the legal situation.

Consequently, according to canon law, provided there was a proper celebration, all marriages, whether or not valid, are considered lawful from the wedding day until the death of one of the parties, or a decree of nullity is issued.

If the Church was capable of making a perfect legal system, we could say that those couples whom God has united in marriage would have valid marriages, and those couples whom God has not united would have invalid marriages. Such a legal system for marriages would ensure complete fidelity to the words of Christ: "what God has united, man must not divide." Unfortunately, the Church's laws are less than perfect, and contradictions do arise as a result.

It has to be said that many of the canons contained in the Code of canon law are not inventions of the Church; that is, laws written by the Church for its own convenience. Many of the laws which the canons seek to express find their source in nature or divine teaching. These too are embodied in canon law insofar as they affect the Church as a whole or its individual members.

For example, it is naturally assumed that it is wrong for a man to marry his mother, sister or daughter, and for a woman to marry her father, brother or son. This we would consider to be against natural law, but it is also embodied in canon law.

The teachings of Jesus in the Bible on the indissolubility of marriage can be said to be of divine law. However, even natural law, that which finds its source in the nature of things, can be said to be divine law, since God is the creator of all natural things. As far as the Church has discovered and understood these natural and divine laws regarding marriage, they have been embodied in canon law.

Also within canon law, there are certain laws which are termed *merely ecclesiastical*. These laws do not come from God or nature but have been promulgated by the Church to ensure that there is good order and a consistency of practice amongst its members. Except in rare cases, dispensation from these *merely ecclesiastical* laws can be given by a bishop. This dispensation will readily be given when the law, in a particular case, stands in the way of common sense or natural justice.

An example of a *merely ecclesiastical* law is that a Catholic must marry in the presence of a Catholic priest, deacon or other appropriately delegated person. However, because this is not a matter of God's law, a dispensation to marry before a non-Catholic minister can be given. If, for example, a Catholic wished to marry a Methodist in the church where the Methodist regularly practised, a dispensation could be granted for the Catholic to marry without a Catholic minister needing to be present.

This law, stating that Catholics must marry before a Catholic minister of religion, came into existence at a time when relations between the Catholic Church and other Christian denominations were at a low ebb. Marriages between a Catholic and a non-Catholic baptised person, called "marriages of mixed religion", were discouraged because of the social and religious problems that could arise. The Church felt it appropriate to safeguard the faith of the

Catholic by insisting that, for such marriages to be valid, a Catholic minister of religion should be present. In this way, it was assumed that the minister would be given the opportunity to instruct the Catholic party about possible future difficulties.

This insistence by the Church on the presence of a Catholic minister of religion is actually beyond natural law. According to the Roman Catholic Church's understanding of the sacrament of marriage, the minister is not essential for the marriage to come into existence. The minister of the sacrament is not the priest or deacon, but it is the man and woman who administer the sacrament to one another. The priest or deacon acts as an official witness, besides any other role such as conducting the ceremony.

It is not without significance that the first reference to marriage in the Bible is found as early as the second chapter of the Book of Genesis: "... a man leaves his father and mother and joins himself to his wife, and they become one body" (*Genesis* 2:24). Marriage was a part of creation long before there were any priests or deacons, even if, it might be argued, it did not become a sacrament until raised to that level by Jesus.

Because people have a natural right to marry, the Church will try to ensure that that right is not impeded. If it is possible for two people to marry according to natural law, and it is only ecclesiastical law which is preventing their marriage, then certain provisions are made to allow them to marry in any case. The most obvious example envisaged by canon law is the possibility that a minister will not be available to perform the ceremony. Two people can exchange consent, before witnesses only, in the event of a minister not being available for thirty days, or in a case in which one of the parties is in danger of dying before a minister becomes available.

Unfortunately, it is not always possible to say with certainty whether laws have their origin in nature or are *merely ecclesiastical*. For example, although it can be said with some certainty that the law that a man may not marry his mother is of natural origin, it is not so clear that a man may not marry his aunt or his cousin or his niece. Yet, the Code of canon law says that these people may not marry one another. However, at the same time, it allows for a dispensation to be granted for a man to marry his aunt; a woman, her uncle; or for cousins to marry.

Thus, it would appear that since the law allows a dispensation to be granted, there is at least some uncertainty about whether this law can be said to be of natural origin. It could also be argued that, since a dispensation can be given, the law must be *merely ecclesiastical*. This argument has to be accepted, yet it is nevertheless true that the marriage between a man and his aunt, or between cousins, would tend to lead some people to wonder if such action was outside natural law. In embodying these laws in the Code of canon law, the Church is effectively discouraging such unions, but is not saying they are wrong. Note that a dispensation is not needed for a man to marry the daughter of his cousin, or likewise for a woman to marry the son of her cousin. Such unions are not considered unnatural.

In later chapters, when marriage nullity is discussed, some of the more obvious ways in which there can be an apparent conflict between the Church's laws of marriage and natural justice will be evident. For the time being it is sufficient to recognise that man-made laws (the *merely ecclesiastical* ones already mentioned) will have limitations which will render them unworkable in some circumstances. A good legal system will have safeguards to ensure that injustices do not occur at such times.

It can truly be said, then, that the Church's laws on marriage are complex. Over the years, a framework of laws and procedures has been developed which tries to recognise both the sacramentality of marriage and its form as a relationship of love between two people. The Church considers these laws to be of the utmost importance, affecting the very heart of marriage in such a way that if certain laws are broken, the marriage simply does not come into existence. This is the starting point for marriage nullity.

Chapter Five

What Is a Declaration of Nullity?

Some marriages don't work. At the present time in England, some 35 to 40% of marriages end in divorce. This proportion is the same even for Catholic marriages. Many attempts have been made to explain why so many marriages break down, ranging from a new malaise in society which simply makes divorce both easy and acceptable, to the fact that married people are looking for fulfilment in marriage, and if they don't find it they will go elsewhere. Whatever the general reason for the increase in the rate of divorce, it does seem clear that people are no longer putting up with a bad marriage.

One result of the increasing number of marriages breaking down is an increase in the number of people wishing to enter a second marriage. Since Jesus taught that divorce is not possible, the Church simply says that the bond of marriage must remain until death. Only then is remarriage possible for the surviving spouse.

Nevertheless, the Church recognises that despite the presumption that all marriages are valid, it is possible that some are not. The Church allows either party to challenge the presumption of validity of his or her marriage providing the other party is still alive. This is true, even if the challenging party was the apparent cause of the breakdown. In the event of the challenge being upheld, a decree of nullity will be issued. However, in reality, for practical reasons which will be explained later, the Church will often not investigate that challenge until a civil divorce has been obtained.

The concept of nullity can be difficult for many Catholics, especially those who have had little formal teaching about marriage. The first thing the Church teaches about marriage is that it is for life.

However, there is nothing about nullity that challenges this teaching. Except in the rarest of cases, marriage is for life. Nullity does not cancel or break a marriage bond. It declares that the marriage bond was never there in the first place; in other words, that a marriage never actually came into existence. A declaration of nullity is, if you like, a statement that the presumption that all marriages are valid does not hold for the particular marriage which is declared null.

Before going further, it is useful to clarify the meaning of the words marriage and wedding. Assuming it is valid, a marriage exists from the moment of consent being exchanged on the wedding day until the death of one of the parties. The wedding is the ceremony celebrating the marriage coming into existence.

Thus, a definition of marriage nullity (commonly referred to as "an annulment") might be:

> A declaration of nullity is a declaration by the competent authority that, at the time of the wedding, there was present some defect which prevented the marriage coming into existence.

This can be a difficult concept to grasp. A marriage is a living relationship of two people, but it is not something which is easily identifiable as a marriage distinct from other relationships. For this reason, we seek to show its existence in such ways as exchanging wedding rings, issuing a certificate, having a special public ceremony and adopting the same surname. These signs all assist us in feeling and believing that the marriage has begun, but they do not actually determine the existence of the marriage. On the wedding day, everyone is led to believe that the marriage comes into existence, but nobody can actually prove that it has in reality, because a marriage is not a tangible entity. The belief which everybody holds on the wedding day, and thereafter, is actually false if the marriage is later declared invalid.

Nevertheless, the belief that a marriage exists is supported by the law, which presumes that the marriage is valid and therefore presumes that it actually exists. Consequently, whether or not it does actually exist, the couple are entitled to all the privileges and rights which the law bestows on married couples, and any children born of that marriage are born within the law; that is, they are legitimate. Thus, even if the marriage does not exist, the law gives the couple and any children the same status as if the marriage did exist. A subsequent declaration of nullity has the effect of taking away the protection of the law *from the date of the declaration.* Thus, even if the marriage is declared null, the couple are recognised as having been legally married from the wedding day to the date of the declaration of nullity.

A declaration of nullity can be made only by the competent authority, who is the diocesan bishop or the Holy Father or somebody acting under his authority.

The declaration is made in the form of a decree; that is, a document which states the fact of the nullity and actually causes it to become law. As such, it is an important document and so is usually retained by the diocese for safe-keeping. The fact of the nullity will be communicated to the priests who have charge of the registers of baptism and reception so that an entry can be made against the record of the marriage.

It is important to understand that, although the decree causes the fact of the nullity to become law, it does not actually make the marriage invalid; in the same way that a marriage certificate does not bring a marriage into existence, but is simply the legal document which confirms the existence of the marriage in law.

In the above definition, the phrase "at the time of the wedding" is very important. The wedding ceremony is the time when a marriage comes into existence. The declaration of nullity refers back to that time and states that although the law presumed that the marriage came into existence, that presumption was false. Hence, a declaration of nullity amounts to a statement of fact. It reverses a legal presumption, but it does not change the fact. It is revealing a truth which was previously hidden.

Because a declaration of nullity can be made only by the competent authority, even if people believe a marriage to be invalid, until it is actually declared so by that authority, the presumption remains in force. For example, it is a part of Church law that a man must be sixteen before he can enter a valid marriage. If, after the marriage ceremony, it was discovered that the man was only fifteen, it would be easy for either party to the marriage to obtain a declaration of nullity. However, until that declaration is obtained, the presumption that the marriage is valid remains in force, and neither party would be free to partake in another marriage ceremony. The invalidity in such a case could be easily proved by producing the appropriate certificates of birth and marriage.

Another example might involve a woman who enters marriage with a most obnoxious man. After attempting to make their marriage work for a few years, she finally decides she has to leave him for her own sanity. In her heart she knows that they never had a proper marital relationship. Nevertheless, she would have to obtain a declaration of nullity before being allowed to enter a second union which would be recognised by the Church.

It could be argued that the necessity for this woman to have to wait for a declaration of nullity is a deprivation of her right to enter a true marriage. Why should she have to wait for a formal declaration of something which, in her heart, she already knows to be? This question has already been examined in a previous chapter. The need for the Church to know the marital status of all people, not just Catholics, comes from a need in any society for order. Without some formal control over the marital status of people, the Church might have difficulty in applying the teaching of Christ about permanence. It also seems right that the formality of having a marriage declared invalid should be treated with at least the same gravity as bringing a marriage into existence. Both have very serious consequences for the couple and for the Church as a whole.

The definition of nullity enables a distinction to be made between nullity and divorce. A common statement made by those who find distasteful the idea of marriage nullity in the Catholic Church is that it is simply another word for divorce. However, a nullity is a declaration that a marriage never came into existence; that is, that what was there did not meet the Church's requirements for a valid marriage. A divorce, on the other hand, legally dissolves a marriage, thereby implicitly assuming the presence of a valid marriage. In English civil law, a divorce can always eventually be obtained. In canon law, a declaration of nullity is often not possible.

Since a declaration of nullity is a statement that, even though a couple performed a wedding ceremony, a marriage never actually came into existence, an understanding of how a marriage comes into existence is fundamental to an understanding of nullity.

Here again, canon law provides a definition which appears too simple in relation to the underlying reality of two people growing together in a relationship of love and making a permanent commitment to one another. Nevertheless, it contains all the elements which are essential for the validity of a marriage, and hence is fundamental to an understanding of marriage nullity.

The first part of canon 1057 says:

> A marriage is brought into existence by the lawfully manifested consent of persons who are legally capable.

This definition forms the basis of the discussion of the next few chapters, and is vital to an understanding of what follows. It contains three essential elements without which the marriage does not come into existence.

Consent is the basis upon which a marriage is brought into existence; that is, each party agreeing to enter marriage with the other. This consent must be *lawfully manifested*; that is, given or expressed in a way which the law determines. It can be given only by people who are *legally capable* of giving that consent. If any of these three elements is missing, the marriage, according to the Catholic Church, is potentially capable of being declared invalid. For it actually to be declared invalid, it is required that one of the parties requests an investigation for invalidity, and that the required proof be available.

Before proceeding with a discussion of the reasons why marriages can be declared invalid, it is necessary to warn the reader of potential dangers:

- For those in a stable marriage: remember that even if a marriage is technically invalid, the Church presumes that all marriages are valid. A long-lasting, wonderfully happy marriage can technically be invalid, but this does not prevent God bestowing every blessing at His disposal on to it. Hence, even if you think your marriage might be invalid, it is presumed valid.
- For those who have suffered marriage breakdown, whether or not separated, *do not assume that you can obtain a declaration of nullity just because you have read something here which suggests your marriage might be invalid.* A declaration of nullity of a marriage is a most serious matter, and it will only be granted when it has been proved with moral certainty that the marriage is invalid.

Chapter Six
Lawful Manifestation

One of the most common misconceptions about the celebration of marriage is that a marriage celebrated in a register office is not recognised by the Church. This will generally only be true if one of the parties is a Catholic. If neither party is a Catholic and the couple were free to marry, the Church will recognise the marriage.

If consent to a marriage, in which one of the parties is a Catholic, is not manifested in a manner recognised by canon law, the marriage can later be declared invalid. The Church sets down strict guidelines for Catholics as to how their marriages should be celebrated. The manner in which consent must be exchanged is called the "form" of marriage. Consent not manifested in the prescribed manner renders the marriage invalid by reason of "defect of form".

Canon law says that marital consent must be exchanged before a priest or deacon. However, in certain circumstances, a lay person can be delegated if a priest or deacon cannot be present. In fact, the law is rather strict about which priest or deacon can conduct the ceremony. For example, a parish priest may always conduct marriages in his own parish, but a visiting priest may do so only with the permission of the parish priest or the bishop of the diocese.

There is much confusion and ignorance about this law of form, and yet it can be easily understood if two things are remembered. The first is that some laws of the Catholic Church, those which are *merely ecclesiastical* (i.e. not of divine origin), apply only to Catholics. This law of form is one such law. Thus, two non-Catholics can, as far as the Catholic Church is concerned, exchange consent before anyone they choose. They are not bound by the Catholic law on form.

This, then, means that the Church recognises as valid all marriages in which neither party is a Catholic, providing that the parties were in all other ways free to marry. Thus, the marriage of two non-Catholics who held their wedding ceremony in a register office would be recognised as valid, as would the marriage of a Baptist and an Anglican exchanging consent in an Anglican church, and the wedding of two Jews in a synagogue. Because none of these people are Catholics, they do not have to have a Catholic minister present when they exchange consent.

The second point to remember is that, for Catholics, it is not the place of marriage which is important but the presence of the appropriate minister. As *merely ecclesiastical* law, the law of form can be put aside if there is a good reason for doing so. It is, for example, sometimes possible, when an intended spouse has a strong affiliation with another Christian Church, for the Catholic party to obtain permission for the wedding to be held in the spouse's church, without the need for a Catholic minister to be present. Also, as explained in a previous chapter, in circumstances when a priest or deacon cannot be present, the law allows a Catholic to exchange consent if there is a danger of death or a qualified priest, deacon or lay person will not be available for thirty or more days.

The law of form can appear complicated, but it is simply summarised thus:

> It can generally be assumed that, if at least one of the parties was a Catholic and the marriage was celebrated in a Catholic church, the marriage is valid. It may only be celebrated elsewhere with permission.
>
> It can generally be assumed that, if neither party is a Catholic, the marriage is valid.

It has to be remembered that this is only referring to the form of celebration. It is only a rule of thumb and there are certain exceptions which are beyond the scope of this book.

The purpose of the law of form within the Church is obviously felt to justify its existence. From the point of view of safeguarding the sacramentality of marriage, the law would seem to serve a useful purpose. There is no doubt that it sometimes causes difficulties for engaged couples of mixed religion. However, with permission now being granted more readily for Catholics to marry in the church of the other party, the difficulty is not nearly as acute as it was some years ago.

The law of form and its invalidating force does not fit easily into canon law as a whole, and it creates some anomalous situations in the case of marriage breakdown. Consider, for example, the case of a Catholic who has not practised his faith for years and who, therefore, decides to marry his non-Catholic fiancée in a register office. The marriage is reasonably happy for twenty years and produces three children. The couple then, for whatever reason, decide to separate and divorce. The man then meets a Catholic for whom the faith is important and they decide to marry. Canon law would enable him to marry in the Catholic church, since he would easily be able to have his first marriage declared null because of lack of form.

This is in sharp contrast to the situation which would have prevailed had he married the first time in a Catholic church, or if he had not been a Catholic. In either of these two latter cases, it would have to be shown that his first marriage was invalid because of some other defect before he could marry the second woman in the Church. Hence, in some circumstances, canon law gives the impression that the Church gives more favourable treatment to a Catholic who married in a register office than to one who married in a church.

From the spiritual point of view, too, the law creates the impression that God will seemingly bless the marriages of those Catholics who marry in church, whilst withholding His grace from those Catholics who marry in a register office. It is only fair to state that this is an unfortunate consequence of the law of form, and is not by any means intended. It is an area of canon law which may well be due for change.

Chapter Seven
Legal Capability

For a marriage to come into existence, both parties have to be legally capable of marrying at the time of the ceremony. In the United Kingdom, and in many other countries, it would be very rare for a marriage to be celebrated by someone who is not legally capable. Those who are not legally capable are said to be impeded, and the circumstance which makes the person incapable is called an impediment.

The reason it is rare for an impeded person to take part in a wedding ceremony is that most impediments are public knowledge. Furthermore, before a wedding takes place, both parties will have signed a declaration stating that they are free from all impediments to the marriage. Even then, at the time of the wedding, before they exchange consent, each party is asked to state that he or she is not aware of any impediment to marriage.

Many impediments in canon law are obvious and instantly recognisable. Others are not so obvious. Some impediments are of divine or natural law, and others contain elements which can be said to be of both divine and *merely ecclesiastical* law. The various impediments are:

Age

A man may not marry before he is sixteen and a woman before she is fourteen. Most people would agree that it is a part of natural law to have some minimum age for marriage, and when girls as young as eight can become pregnant, perhaps this is nature's way of saying they should be able to marry at that age. The Church, by setting an age of fourteen for girls and sixteen for boys, recognises that physical development is only a part of the general development of the person.

The actual ages of fourteen and sixteen are a matter of ecclesiastical law, and permission can in theory be granted for marriage at an earlier age. The age difference between the sexes would appear to be in recognition of the fact that girls seem to mature at an earlier age than boys.

The law is so worded here that it makes it clear that these ages are minimal. All women aged less than fourteen and all men aged less than sixteen are unable to enter a valid marriage. This means that a person who is slightly older than the minimum is not necessarily capable of entering a valid marriage. Such a marriage would be presumed by canon law to be valid. Nevertheless, the law implies by its wording that a person who marries when only slightly older than the minimum might well give invalid consent. The older the person, the less is the possibility of this happening.

Impotence

The ability to have sexual intercourse is of vital importance to a marriage, to the extent that if a couple cannot have intercourse because of a problem in either one, or even which is relative to the couple, the marriage could be declared invalid. Note that it is *impotence* that is invalidating and not *sterility*.

Previous Marriage

This is perhaps the most obvious impediment. Since marriage is for life, and the bond of marriage between two people continues until one dies, an impediment to another marriage always arises as soon as one marriage is celebrated. If the first marriage is later declared to have been invalid, the impediment of previous marriage is obviously cancelled.

Non-baptism

The marriage of a pagan to a Catholic is considered to be potentially harmful to the faith of the Catholic and certain conditions must be fulfilled before the marriage can validly be entered. These conditions refer to the upbringing of children and the preservation of the faith of the Catholic party.

Holy Orders

Apart from married permanent deacons, the clergy all make a promise of celibacy when they enter the clerical state. A permanent deacon who is married cannot remarry if his wife dies. Special permission is sometimes given for a married man to be ordained to the priesthood. These restrictions on marriage are of ecclesiastical law.

Religious Vows

Anyone who has taken a public, perpetual vow of chastity in a religious institute cannot validly enter marriage.

Abduction

A woman who has been abducted with a view to marriage and remains captive is impeded from entering marriage. The law does not envisage the situation in which a man is abducted.

Murder

Everyone consents to marriage "till death do us part". In order to discourage those who wish to remarry from murdering the first spouse, the Church makes the second marriage invalid. This is true whether it is the married person who does the killing, or the intended spouse, or a third party hired by either spouse.

Blood Relationship

Marriage is not possible between a person and his or her direct ancestor or descendant. Thus, a woman may not marry her father, grandfather, son or grandson. Nor is marriage possible between brothers and sisters. This is true whether they have both parents in common, or only one. Special permission is needed to marry other close relations such as aunts, uncles, cousins or great aunts and uncles.

Relationship by Marriage

It is not possible to marry the natural parents or children of your deceased spouse. Thus, Andrew marries widow Brenda, who has a daughter from her first husband. If Brenda died, Andrew could not marry either Brenda's daughter or Brenda's mother even though he is not naturally related to either. However, if Brenda had a sister who was free to marry, there would be no reason why Andrew and she could not marry.

Public Propriety

Common law husbands and wives are treated for some purposes in the same way as though the couple had actually married. Hence, if Jack and Wendy are living together and are considered man and wife even though they have never exchanged consent, Jack cannot then marry Wendy's mother or daughter.

Adoption

When a legal relationship is established by adoption, an impediment to marriage arises between the adopted person and the adopting parents and grandparents, and any natural children of those parents.

Note that it is rare for any marriage to be declared invalid because of the presence of an impediment, since most impediments would be known before marriage. However, while it is possible that an impediment, say of relationship, might be discovered after the wedding ceremony, the only impediment which might properly only be discovered after marriage is that of impotence.

Chapter Eight
Consent

It will have become clear from the last two chapters that a marriage can be declared invalid for some fairly obvious reasons. Of all the possible grounds for nullity described so far, the most common reason for granting a decree of nullity is that one of the parties was a Catholic and the wedding was celebrated in a register office.

Why a Catholic should choose to marry in a register office is not clear. However, it is certain that some people are unaware that the Church does not recognise such a ceremony as bringing a marriage into existence. Others marry in a register office because there is some impediment which would mean that they could not marry in a church; for example, a nun who had left the convent to marry and who had not yet been released from her vow of chastity. Clearly this could only happen if they were free to marry according to civil law but not according to canon law. Others have simply lost their faith, or have not been to church for so long that they would feel hypocritical marrying in church.

The invalidity of a marriage because of lack of form or the presence of an impediment can be easily proved. The only exception to this might be the impediment of impotence, which might not be discovered until after the wedding. If an application for nullity did involve impotence, it might have to be treated in the same way as a case involving a *defect of consent*.

Marriages invalid by reason of a *defect of consent* are much more difficult to prove. Yet, perhaps the majority of applications for marriage nullity are processed under this general heading of *defect of consent*. Consequently, it is necessary to study in some detail the grounds for nullity under this heading. These grounds form the subject matter of the remaining chapters of this section.

In the wedding ceremony, after announcing his or her intention to take the other, each says: "I take thee to be my lawful wedded wife/husband." This is the moment of consent. In this act, two things are presumed: that the intention of each spouse actually conforms to what is being said, and that each is capable of giving valid consent to marriage. It is in showing that there is a serious defect of intention or a serious defect of capability that a marriage can be declared invalid because of a defect in the consent of the parties.

Before examining the most common grounds for nullity under this heading of *defect of consent*, the following examples will give something of the flavour of how this consent might be defective.

A story appeared in the national press a few years ago of an American tourist who was visiting England for the first time. She had collected a car at the airport and driven off to enjoy her visit. After three days she brought the car back complaining that it was too noisy and was consuming vast amounts of fuel, far too much for the mileage she was doing. When a mechanic tried the car, he could find no fault. When he invited the woman to drive it again with him as a passenger, he discovered that she drove everywhere in first gear. The woman had simply never driven a car with a manual gearbox, having learned in and always driven one with an automatic gearbox.

Probably the woman had never seen herself as being unable to drive some cars. Before coming to England she would always have answered affirmatively to any enquiry about her ability to drive. However, on going back to the States, she would probably have learned enough to qualify her response to such an enquiry. She had learned that her ability to drive was restricted to cars with automatic gears. Had she thought that she would have been incapable of driving the car she would be given on arrival in England, she would not have ordered one, or at least ensured that she ordered one with an automatic gearbox.

We can all make relationships, but only once during the lifetime of most of us do we actually agree to form a marital relationship. No matter whether we have been prepared simply by the experience of living, or have set out deliberately to know and understand as far as possible what being married means, actually entering the married state is a new experience which can potentially be very different from expectations.

The decision to enter marriage is a decision for life. In order that two people do so validly, canon law demands that those who enter marriage at least know what they are doing. However, the level of knowledge required is absolutely basic. The appropriate canon [Canon 1096] says:

> . . .it is necessary that the contracting parties be at least not ignorant of the fact that marriage is a permanent partnership between a man and a woman, ordered to the procreation of children through some form of sexual co-operation.

It can still happen, even today, that a person will be a party to a wedding ceremony without having any realistic knowledge of how children are procreated. Anyone who can show to the Church's satisfaction that he or she had some vague notion that holding hands and kissing would result in children being born would possibly be able to receive a declaration of nullity.

This may seem an extreme case, but many older people will recall that the sex education they received in school or at home was, if anything, minimal. Many people went into marriage with only a vague notion of how two bodies become one, and would have to admit that their first attempts at intercourse succeeded more by good luck than judgment. However, they could not claim they were ignorant that marriage required some form of sexual co-operation. So this canon is talking of an ignorance of the most basic sexual knowledge.

Another ground under which a declaration of nullity can be granted is when it can be proved that a person lacks sufficient use of reason. This differs from the previous ground. In both cases, it can be said that the person did not know what he or she was doing. However, under the previous ground, an otherwise normal person was simply ignorant. The latter ground concerns the case when a person gives consent whilst being of unsound mind.

Note that it is the moment of consent which is important. Hence, a person might temporarily lack the use of reason whilst being quite reasonable at other times. If this person lacked a sufficient use of reason at the moment of giving consent, and this could be proved to the satisfaction of the Church, the marriage could be declared invalid.

What exactly constitutes a lack of the use of reason could form the basis of a lengthy debate. Many a father has stood in church and wondered if his daughter has lost her use of reason in her choice of partner. This thinking, whilst of great concern to the father, would not be acceptable to the appropriate ecclesiastical authorities. The lack of objectivity in such an opinion would be something of a handicap to the required proof. Nevertheless, worried fathers might find some comfort if they read on.

The Church is concerned here that people entering marriage do so in the fullest possible (not necessarily full) awareness of the commitment they are undertaking. Many things can deprive a person of a sufficient use of reason. The man who has had a few drinks before arriving at the church might have done enough damage to invalidate his consent. However, since lacking sufficient use of reason is such a vague phrase, it would be difficult to prove that he had drunk sufficient to deprive him of the ability to give valid consent. If it was to be argued that he lacked a sufficient use of reason, it would be envisaged that his behaviour in the circumstances would be unreasonable; that is, that he did not treat the ceremony or those present with the respect and dignity which was deserved.

Other factors that could temporarily affect a person's sufficient use of reason could be drugs, some temporary illness, fainting, delirium, an epileptic fit, or even excessive sleepiness. It should be said that although these factors are likely to prevent consent from being valid, they are actually far more likely to prevent consent being given at all, since the affected person will almost certainly be unable to express the words of consent. The most likely outcome for some of these examples would be that consent would be delayed until the person recovered from the fit or faint.

The much more difficult cases to deal with under this ground concern the marriage of those who are judged permanently to lack the use of reason. It would be extremely difficult, and almost certainly unwise, to prejudge the marriages of those who might lack the use of reason and attempt to prevent such a marriage taking place. What, for example, is to be done in the case of two people who are of such limited intellect that they have always lived in institutions? Would anyone have the right to suggest they should not be able to marry if that is what they wanted? In the protected environment of the institution the marriage might survive. Even if it did not, the chances of either wishing to challenge the validity of the marriage would probably be slim. This might not be the case if only one of the parties could be said to lack the sufficient use of reason.

In fact, both of these grounds, whilst creating possibilities for declarations of nullity, are rarely quoted as the reasons for which a marriage is declared invalid. The most common ground is that of lack of due discretion, which is the subject matter of the next three chapters.

Chapter Nine
Lack of Due Discretion (1)

From the earliest years of intelligent life each of us is making thousands of decisions every day. All of these decisions involve an intricate process of thought, evaluation and judgment.

Take the simple decision to cross the road. It involves a number of decisions. "Do I want to cross the road? Why do I want to cross the road? Do I want to cross now or further on? Is it safe to cross now? Would I be safer to cross after the bus has passed or before? Can I run across if I need to get there more quickly than anticipated? Will I have to run if I cross now? Do I want to make that effort? Is there anybody on the other side who I would rather avoid? Is there anything I need to do on this side first?" Some or all of these questions need to be addressed before the act of crossing is made.

Similarly, there are many decisions involved in buying a pair of shoes: are they the right colour, price, shape, style, fabric, size or comfort? Can I bring them back if I am not happy with them when I get home? If I have a deep social conscience, or have an interest in the shoe industry: where are they made, who by, and using what materials?

These are just two frequently made decisions which illustrate something of the complexity of thought and evaluative processes involved in making decisions. It is not difficult to see that the more insignificant the decision, the less is the need to spend time thinking about, evaluating and judging the pros and cons of the decision. On a scale of important decisions in life, crossing the road and buying a pair of shoes would appear quite far down. For many people, the decision to marry would be very near, if not at, the top of the scale. It is, after all, a decision with lifelong consequences. It is not a decision which can be easily put aside if a mistake is made. As a decision with such grave consequences, the extent of thought, evaluation and judgment which accompanies the decision must be proportionately greater than that required for more mundane decisions. It stands to reason, therefore, that a person proposing to enter marriage must have a minimal knowledge of the rights and obligations which are attached to the marriage covenant, and an awareness of the nature of that covenant.

It is also obvious that, when a man and a woman consent to form a marriage, the intention of each is to form that marriage with one specific person. Consent is not given merely to enter the marital state. Consent is given to enter the married state with one other specific person. The marriage ceremony indicates this when the man is asked if he takes this named woman; and the woman this named man. The marriage covenant is not between a man and any woman; nor between a woman and any man.

The marriage promises are made to the intended spouse and not to the world at large. Except for the parties, those present take only the role of witness to the exchange of promises. There is no sense in which they receive those promises. Thus, it is impossible to talk of matrimonial rights and obligations for a specific marriage, without considering those rights and obligations with respect to specific persons. Hence, an important element in the giving of consent is a minimum knowledge of the person to whom consent is being given.

Canon law, then, recognises that the decision to form a marriage covenant with another person must be made after a period of discernment; that is, a period of interior thought and questioning about the proposed marriage. During this period of discernment, certain questions should have been asked by each person, and a judgment made as to whether or not marriage is appropriate. Each partner will have asked himself or herself: Am I prepared to enter a lifelong partnership with this person? Am I prepared to be faithful to this person "till death us do part"? Am I prepared to attempt to bring children into the world with this person, and to help to educate these children in all aspects of life, assuming that age or some other factor does not make this impossible? Am I prepared to conduct my life with this person in such a way that I will consider not only my own needs, but also the needs of my spouse; that is, in a way that will foster our mutual well-being? While these questions may well not be formulated so specifically during the period of discernment – indeed they may be very vague – the general concepts contained herein must underlie the decision to marry.

Put very simply, each party to a marriage should have some knowledge of what is required, and have begun to see himself or herself in that role of husband or wife to the proposed spouse. We would say that a person who has done this possesses "due discretion of judgment". The ground for nullity is usually referred to simply as "lack of due discretion".

However, not only must this evaluation underlie the decision to marry, but the person concerned must also possess the ability to put those concepts into practice. Any lack of ability, in itself, could form a basis for the use of the separate ground of "inability", which is discussed later (Chapter 12). However, due discretion of judgment is concerned with the person's self-perception, and demands a certain self-knowledge (and, by implication, an ability to make a realistic appraisal of the self). Again, perfect self-knowledge is not required, but it is required that a person be able to judge, to some extent, his or her own fitness for the marriage covenant.

Thus, the question is not only am I *prepared* to be faithful to this person for life, but am I also *able* to be faithful to this person for life? Likewise, am I *able* to give of myself for life to this person? Am I *able* to attempt to bring children into the world and to help to educate them? Am I *able* to conduct my life with this person in a way which will foster our mutual well-being?

The majority of people would probably not hesitate to answer affirmatively to these questions, but there is no doubt that some people have personality disorders which would make it impossible for them to form a true marital relationship. Hence, anyone who is aware of a facet of his personality which would seriously affect his ability to form a marital relationship would have to consider the effect of this as part of the premarital evaluation process. It is, for example, well known that alcoholism can seriously affect a marriage. The failure of an alcoholic to evaluate the effect of his addiction on a forthcoming marriage might well render his consent invalid.

It is apparent, then, that each person's premarital thought and evaluation process must focus on three things: the intended spouse, his or her own ability, and the nature of the marital relationship. A failure to carry out this preparation process might cause the marriage to be invalid.

Note that this process would, for most people, be common sense. What is required here is nothing more than the natural process of evaluation before any major decision. It is true that some people will take this preparation far more seriously than others. Some couples attend special courses for the engaged which are designed so that the couples have plenty of time to discuss their own expectations of marriage. The more conscientious will probably also leave plenty of time between the engagement and the wedding. That time will be spent getting to know the other and planning for the future. It is a time when some fundamental differences can emerge. Better to find out about these and come to some compromise before the wedding, than discover after the wedding that neither is prepared to give way.

In a limited number of cases, this period of preparation can be tortuous, especially if there are particular doubts about the proposed union. These doubts will often not be discussed with the other (for fear of upsetting him/her), and may well be suppressed if there is nobody close enough to whom they might be revealed. As the wedding day approaches and more and more commitments are made – the reception, cars, church, and honeymoon are all booked, the bride has bought her dress and the groom has arranged the hire of his suit – it becomes more and more difficult to halt the proceedings and admit that something is wrong. Even if one does admit to the other that he or she wants to call off the wedding, the distress of the other, sometimes accompanied by pleadings and tears, can be enough to force a change of mind in the doubting partner. It is a brave person who will admit that a mistake has been made and that the wedding is not to take place.

Such doubts can easily occupy a person's mind much more than thoughts of the future. Pre-marriage conversations with the intended spouse about their future will become stilted and brief. In times of such anxiety, when the person is deeply worried about the promises that are to be made on the wedding day, it is unlikely that much thought will be given to the longer term consequences of the marriage. Each person must make a free decision, and that freedom is eroded if one is putting pressure on the other to marry more quickly than is wanted; or worse, pressure to marry at all. Such circumstances could lead to the doubting partner giving invalid consent.

From what has been said so far of this ground of lack of due discretion, it will have become obvious that these are mental processes; a mixture of thoughts and feelings occurring during the period of courtship and engagement. It might seem strange, then, that the Church is able to use this ground to declare marriages invalid. After all, how can it be shown what goes on in a person's mind before the exchange of consent on the wedding day?

The truth is that nobody can know with certainty the mental processes that accompany the decision to marry. The Church proves lack of due discretion in much the same way that a person is found guilty in a court of law because of circumstantial evidence. A man is found dead, and the fatal bullet was fired from Mr X's gun, retrieved from a nearby ditch, with only his fingerprints on it. Mr X was seen in the area at the time. He cannot account for his movements, and he has no alibi. He is shown to have a motive for killing the man. There is a good chance that Mr X will be found guilty, even though he denies the charge and nobody witnessed the shooting. From the circumstantial evidence alone, there is reasonable certainty that Mr X pulled the trigger.

Before examining in detail how this evidence can prove a lack of due discretion, it is worthwhile addressing the question that always arises at talks given on this topic: surely everyone can be said to have lacked due discretion of judgment for marriage, for nobody knows what they are doing when they enter marriage? Marriage, after all, involves a lifetime of discovery of the other person, the self and the commitment involved in the relationship.

This ground for nullity must not be taken out of context. It is true that nobody has perfect knowledge of the commitment they are undertaking. The law requires that it be shown that there was a "grave" lack of discretion of judgment before the ground can be cited as the reason for nullity. Although a definition of what constitutes grave is not given, it is clear that the law envisages something which is extraordinary, or beyond normal.

Chapter Ten
Lack of Due Discretion (2)

The range of evidence which might prove a marriage invalid because of a grave lack of discretion of judgment is extremely wide, as will be realised by the examples given in this chapter. It is impossible to set precise standards by stating that some circumstances will make a marriage invalid and others will not. Each case is judged on its own merit and two similar sets of circumstances will produce two different results when the marriage is tested for validity. For this reason, great care must be taken that definite conclusions for one marriage are not drawn from the circumstances of another. Many different factors come into play when a marriage is examined and the weight which is attached to particular circumstances could be different for every case.

An example will help. The general difference in maturity and experience of life between a twenty-four year old and a seventeen year old will be quite marked. While both are above the legal limit beyond which it is not presumed that the marriage is invalid (fourteen for women; sixteen for men), it can be said with some degree of certainty that a seventeen year old, man or woman, is unlikely to have experienced enough of human relationships and life in general to be making a free choice in marrying at that age. The fact that he or she is seventeen is not in itself sufficient to declare the marriage invalid, and many a marriage in which one of the parties was seventeen will have been truly blessed by God. However, in the event of the breakdown of a marriage involving a person of young age, if circumstances show that there were other factors for considering the marriage invalid, the fact of the youthfulness of the man or woman at the time of the marriage might sway the decision in favour of nullity.

When Anthony was eighteen and Cleopatra was seventeen, they met at a youth club and very quickly fell in love. This was the first real romance for each. They had very little in common, but having a romantic relationship made each feel good and gave them status among their friends.

Anthony wanted Cleopatra to have full sexual relations with him. She was reluctant, but was afraid she would lose him if she refused. One evening, when they were babysitting for her elder sister, she gave in to his pressure. Two months later, she began to think she was pregnant, and she related her fears to Anthony. His reaction was disbelief and they agreed to say nothing until the pregnancy was confirmed.

By the time it was confirmed, they had discussed the likely reaction of their parents. Cleopatra knew that her parents would not easily accept her as a single mother. Anthony felt that he should "do the honourable thing" and marry her. By the time they told their parents, they had virtually made the decision to marry, and the parents were only too willing to see the wedding take place as soon as possible.

The marriage lasted for five years before Cleopatra could take no more. Problems began from the moment they set up home together. Anthony would come home from work, have his tea and go out with his friends. At first, he came home at a reasonable time, but after the birth of their son, he started coming home later.

They never talked at a serious level, and any time that Cleopatra tried to talk to him, they would argue and he would storm out. Several times she discovered that he had spent the night at his parents' home rather than face her. Eventually they decided to part, and divorced several years later. When Cleopatra, a Catholic, decided she would want to remarry if she ever met the right man, she applied for a declaration that her marriage to Anthony was invalid.

Many factors would be taken into consideration if this marriage was to be examined for possible invalidity. The most important of these would be that the couple seemingly only married at that time because Cleopatra was pregnant. Neither appears to have thought of the possibility that their relationship would end in marriage, even though Cleopatra would admit that the idea had crossed her mind.

She had dismissed it quickly because she did not see herself marrying until at least her early twenties. Anthony can only say that he thought of marriage after Cleopatra told him she was pregnant. After his first reaction of disbelief, he started to have daydreams about his son running around a football field in the colours of his favourite team, and he began to feel proud that he had fathered a future football star. The thought that the baby might be a girl did not cross his mind.

It is obvious that the pregnancy of Cleopatra had a marked effect on the freedom of each in making the decision to marry. Cleopatra seemed concerned to follow that course of action which she perceived her parents would want, and Anthony was concerned that he should at least attempt to stand by Cleopatra, which to him meant marrying her. Each was obviously concerned to do what was expected of him or her, and it is unlikely that either would have given any deep thought to the future. Both were concerned simply that she was pregnant by him and they were not married. Marriage seemed to be their only option.

Furthermore, Anthony's behaviour in the marriage would indicate that he was, at that time at least, unwilling and probably psychologically unable to make that commitment. There seems to have been little realisation of the requirement to attempt to form a community of life with his wife, and his staying out even later after the birth of the child might well indicate an unwillingness to shoulder the responsibility of fatherhood, despite his obvious good intentions at the time of the wedding.

Another element which would be considered is the maturity of the parties. Both were very young at that time of critical decision making. It was the first romantic relationship for each; a time when it can be difficult to distinguish infatuation from genuine feelings of love. The Church would take into account their youthfulness, and might also give some weight to the fact that it was the first relationship for each.

A reflection of the maturity of each at that time is given in the information available. Anthony's fixation on the future football star, and virtual denial of the possibility of the child being female, is unrealistic. It is also relevant that Cleopatra was more concerned with living up to her parents' expectations than she was with making a decision which was right for her. There was a lack of maturity in her failure to break away from the expectations of her parents.

These are just some of the conclusions that might be reached if this marriage was to be examined for invalidity. Care is being taken not to draw definitive conclusions. No marriage can definitely be said to be invalid, unless it is declared as such by the competent authority. Nevertheless, there is a good chance that this marriage would be found to have been invalid.

This example does not mean that all marriages which come into existence on the occasion of a pregnancy can be interpreted as invalid. Many couples have found themselves marrying in such circumstances, and there can be little doubt that many of these marriages have been happy and permanent. Suppose, for example, that Anthony came to realise one day how lucky he was to have a child. Perhaps the first smile of the baby was enough to win his heart. He began to take an active interest in the child and over the years became a true father and a good husband. The validity of his marriage to Cleopatra would never be questioned. Again, it is important to realise that all things are possible to God.

Now consider the following example:

> Adam and Eve were both twenty and had been courting for three years. They had talked about marriage, and twelve months ago became engaged, although they decided that they would wait at least two years before marrying because both were still at college. After their engagement, they had regular sexual relations, but took precautions against pregnancy. However, despite their precautions, Eve became pregnant. As a result, and without consulting anyone, they decided to marry as quickly as possible.

> After one month of marriage Eve miscarried, and both were extremely upset. They bottled up their feelings, not knowing how to express them to one another, and the lack of communication became a wedge between them. After only a few months, Adam told the whole story to another female friend who had always felt attracted to him. He ended up being unfaithful with her and, feeling that he had betrayed Eve and seeing no future in their marriage, he told her that their marriage was over. Several years later, after the divorce, Eve sought to have the marriage declared invalid.

Like Anthony and Cleopatra, Adam and Eve married on the occasion of a pregnancy. However, in the first case, the marriage almost certainly occurred only because of the pregnancy. Whilst it was possible they might have married in the future, it was certainly not envisaged by either before the pregnancy was discovered.

In the case of Adam and Eve, the marriage occurred only *at that time* because of the pregnancy. Whereas the pregnancy did detract from their freedom to wait a little longer, from the information available it cannot be said with any certainty to have deprived them of their freedom of choice of marital partner or of marriage itself, since they had already decided they wanted to marry. The pregnancy, then, cannot be accepted as having any serious bearing on the process of evaluation of the decision to marry. That does not mean that the marriage may not be declared invalid. The Church would need to consider all the other circumstances of the couple and their marriage before making such a decision.

Hence, it can be said that anything which has the effect of depriving a person of the freedom to choose marriage would probably also deprive him or her of the ability to evaluate the decision to marry. Thus, this particular ground of lack of due discretion can be said to overlap the ground of force and fear, about which more will be said later (see Chapter 15).

It will be obvious from all this that a certain maturity and depth of knowledge of life in general, and marriage in particular, is essential for a person to evaluate adequately the decision to marry; for a realistic understanding of the marriage covenant would be necessary before it could be evaluated in relation to a specific person.

It is also obvious, then, that a person ignorant of sexual matters, and particularly the sexual act proper to marriage, would not have a realistic understanding of marriage and would not be able to evaluate the decision to marry in all its essential elements.

Similarly, if a person is brought up in a family in which divorce is commonplace and acceptable, it is possible that he or she would be unable to evaluate marriage in a realistic way; that is, as a permanent relationship which allows separation only as a last resort. The same can be said of anyone entering marriage with a gravely distorted view of any of the rights and obligations of marriage.

Consider the following example:

> Albert is engaged to Priscilla and they have been seeing one another for several nights a week over a two-year period. On the nights he does not see her, he often goes

out with his friends for a drink, but at least once a week he goes to visit another woman. He has been having a sexual relationship with her for some years. He has never told Priscilla about this, as he has never told her of other things about himself.

Even after the wedding, he continues to visit the other woman and to have sexual relations with her. It is only when Priscilla accidentally discovers that he is not with his friends one night that she becomes suspicious. When she confronts him, he lies to her about being with his friends, not knowing that she knows the truth. When he realises that he has been caught out in a lie, he confesses to her about the other woman. When Priscilla finally brings her case to the Church for a declaration of nullity, it transpires that Albert's father is known to have been unfaithful to his wife for many years.

In addition to the possibility of other grounds, it might successfully be argued that Albert did not have a realistic understanding of the concept of fidelity in marriage, and was therefore unable to evaluate properly his decision to marry Priscilla.

A lack of realism can also occur for other reasons. For many people, the first relationship with a member of the opposite sex can be a very traumatic and even bizarre experience. The first sudden realisation of reciprocated feelings for someone who finds you attractive, makes you feel important and special, and says they actually like you, never mind love you, can turn the most sane and sensible being into a quivering, irrational and unreasonable wreck. A slight exaggeration perhaps, but for a while, being with, talking to, listening to and seeing the object of that infatuation can be the only thing on earth that matters. At such times, marriage is certain to be on the agenda.

Fortunately, through the love-sick haze, most people can still grasp enough of reality to recognise the syndrome affecting them, and only a few will actually end up married before the worst of these effects begin to subside. Coming down to earth can be a great shock. In this infatuated condition, it is very difficult to make rational and sensible decisions, and it can be the case that those who do marry under the spell of infatuation will end up regretting the decision.

However, it is not just infatuation that can lead people to be unrealistic. It is not uncommon for someone who has grown up as the offspring of happily married parents to perceive marriage only in terms of that happiness. In their minds, they equate marriage with peace, harmony and love. The idea that some marriages can be unhappy simply does not occur, and the fact that the proposed partner acts in a highly irresponsible manner during the courtship does not worry them. They fail to make an adequate evaluation of the reality of being married to that person.

> Jack and Jill have been courting for twelve months and Jill has known for some years that she wants marriage and then motherhood. Her parents are happily married, and Jill knows that is what she wants for herself. At twenty-three, she has envied for some time her friends who are either already married or who are engaged. Consequently, she has let it be known to Jack that she would like to see their relationship end in marriage.

> Jack is also twenty-three. He is quite happy to give Jill anything she wants because he finds her very attractive and knows that his friends consider him lucky to have Jill as a girlfriend. However, his idea of enjoying himself is to go drinking with his friends, and he frequently drinks to excess. Most of his earnings is spent on drink and he has lost two jobs because he finds it difficult to get up in the morning after a night at the pub. Twice a week he goes out with Jill, but usually he manages to persuade her to spend part of the evening drinking. On these evenings, he tries to restrict his intake, but he has sometimes ended up a little argumentative and has had to apologise to Jill the next day.

> Despite his behaviour, and her friends suggesting to her that he might not be the right person for her, Jill is convinced that everything will be all right once they are married.

> When, after two years of marriage, he has not changed as she hoped, and she has become worn down by his constant drinking, the waste of money, and the absence of emotional input, she admits to herself that she has made a mistake, and leaves him.

Putting aside for the moment the validity or otherwise of Jack's consent, it might well be argued that Jill's consent was invalid. She had been looking at marriage "through rose-coloured spectacles". Because the marriage of her parents was happy, she had naïvely assumed that her own marriage would be the same. However, the more naïve part of her approach to this marriage was her assumption that Jack would change the pattern of his behaviour after they were married. There was certainly a lack of realism in her approach.

However, some people might argue that, at twenty-three, Jill should have known better. Assuming that she was a woman of average intelligence, with no pressure on her other than that she simply wanted to be married and felt envious of her friends who had already achieved that status, it could be argued that she was naïve and did lack discretion of judgment, but that this was not so grave as to invalidate her consent. It is difficult to argue that Jill did not know what she was doing in marrying Jack. She had plenty of time to get to know him and something of his habits and behaviour. Some would say that she married him for better or for worse, and it was her hard luck that she got the worse.

Both arguments seem reasonable. Yet, the fact that Jill, at twenty-three, should have known better does not mean that she did know better. It can be a mistake to assume that normally mature people are able to approach marriage with the same sense of responsibility as they do their job or other relationships. It is possibly the romanticism of marriage which causes some to lack their usual realistic approach, but it is also likely that the nature of the marital relationship is such that inexperience or naïveté will result in a poorly evaluated decision. It is possible to have such confidence in your own ability to tackle most things in life that you forget to be wary when a new experience is encountered.

The suggestion that Jack married Jill "for better, for worse" is taking that phrase out of context. It does not refer to the state of the parties at the time of the wedding. When a couple promise to marry "for better, for worse", they are referring to events which are to befall them in the future, not to the state of things at the time of the wedding. A marriage ceremony brings into existence a partnership intended to foster the well-being of both parties. A marriage which results in one of the parties being worse off than if he or she had remained single is failing to achieve its purpose. It would be nonsense, then, to suggest that a person can marry into a situation which immediately renders him or her worse off. Such a marriage would be fundamentally flawed and very likely invalid. Of course, there is no guarantee about the future, but it seems reasonable to say that, at the time of exchanging consent, there should be at least a realistic potential for fostering the well-being of each.

In reality, however, if Jill applied for a declaration that her marriage to Jack was null and void, the Church would be far more likely to judge her application on the validity or otherwise of Jack's consent which, on the face of it, was most probably invalid.

Chapter Eleven
Lack of Due Discretion (3)

The need to evaluate the decision to marry by taking into account particular conditions such as alcoholism has already been mentioned. The same is true for any special conditions which are present at the time of a proposed marriage. Thus, particular health problems, whether of the mind or body, differences of faith or culture, and unusual habits or traits of personality must form part of the process of evaluation before marriage. It is one thing to know that a potential difficulty will arise in a marriage, but quite another to live with that difficulty twenty-four hours a day, every day. Again, the greater the problem, the more thought and evaluation required.

This same reasoning is true for those who have commitments which cannot be abandoned at the time of the wedding. Consider, for example, a man who has taken on a six year commitment to the Royal Navy. It would be necessary for him and any prospective wife to discuss and examine the effect his commitment would have on their married life.

Long absences are never easy in a marriage, and there is a high proportion of failures when these occur. The pre-marriage discussions of the couple would hopefully also include the possibility that he might wish to renew his commitment at the end of the six year period. He should not do that without his wife's agreement. She had to respect his commitment to the Navy at marriage. However, having made a commitment to her in the form of a gift of himself, his marriage should take precedence over his job, and the decision to sign on for a further period should be a joint decision. If it was not, however, there would not necessarily be any implications for the validity of his consent to marriage.

Commitments to people might also feature in a decision for marriage. The presence of infirm or elderly relatives should be taken into consideration. The partnership that is formed when two lives are joined together must embrace all that is necessarily part of those lives. Much will depend on the extent of dependency. When there is total dependency, most often encountered in the form of a child from a previous relationship, there is a special need for careful evaluation.

> Patricia has a five year old son, Rupert, from her first marriage. Her husband was tragically killed four years ago. She has now met Quentin and they have developed a good and loving relationship. Patricia has been anxious to allow Quentin to meet Rupert, and to watch their interaction. They seem to get on well, and Quentin likes him and entertains him. When he buys presents for Patricia, he is careful also to buy for Rupert. They have been on holiday together, and everything seemed to go well. Although, when Quentin once reprimanded Rupert for hitting another child, Patricia rounded on Quentin in a way which had slightly disturbed him.

> A year later the couple married. They had argued a little about Patricia's insistence that Rupert accompany them on the honeymoon, but Quentin had given way for the sake of peace. He could not understand why Patricia's mother's offer to take him for a week had not been accepted.

> Initially, Quentin's relationship with Patricia was reasonable, but her attitude to his relationship with Rupert was becoming more and more disturbing, and a wedge was developing between them. She would not allow him any say in Rupert's upbringing. When they discussed these matters, it would always be her wishes which prevailed. If Quentin returned from a business trip with a gift for Rupert, it always mysteriously broke within a few days and was thrown away. When he tried to educate or correct Rupert, Patricia would contradict him. Finally, these matters became the subject of arguments between Patricia and Quentin. It was not much longer before they separated.

Again, in this case, there are many factors which come into play. Her particular circumstances would demand that Patricia, in making a gift of herself in marriage, made also a gift of Rupert, who was so united with her that she could not otherwise have made a gift of herself. For some reason she seems not to have made that gift, and it might successfully have been argued that she had failed to evaluate marriage in those terms. The same could not have been argued for Quentin, who does appear to have evaluated his decision in terms of a gift of himself to both Patricia and to Rupert. Had he failed to take on his role of adoptive father – perhaps by seeing Rupert as a hindrance or unwanted responsibility – it might also be argued that he had failed to evaluate his decision to marry.

This example is a good illustration of how the failure of one party to evaluate the nature of marriage can be manifest in the behaviour of that party after the wedding, without any manifestation of that failure during the courtship. However, not all such failures can necessarily be taken as proof of a lack of discretionary judgment, and it is only a grave lack which would invalidate a marriage. People do not become perfect husbands or wives overnight, and the process of adapting to the role of spouse is lifelong. The behaviour of one spouse might clash with the other's expectations, and the nature of the marriage covenant, expressed in the gift of self, calls for discussion, compromise and even sacrifice.

It is useful to list some typical examples of behaviour which might cause disturbance in a marriage, and which might indicate a failure to recognise the true nature of marriage. However, it must be remembered that this behaviour in itself does not cause a marriage to be invalid. First the list, and then further discussion:

- Socialising without reference to the other.
- Selfishness with money or possessions.
- Decision making without reference to the other.
- Taking problems to others rather than partner.
- Inappropriate interaction with others (e.g. excessive flirtation).
- Unwillingness to discuss, compromise, or see other's point of view.
- Selfishness in the sexual act.
- Failure to take a fair share of responsibilities (e.g. household chores).
- Excessive time spent at work or activities which exclude the other.
- Unwillingness to have children, or to share the responsibility of children.

The one thing that all of these have in common (except perhaps the unwillingness to have children) is that they detract from the partnership aspect of marriage by not taking into account the needs of the spouse. In some marriages, certain elements of this behaviour will be quite acceptable, and there will be no question of the behaviour creating problems or leading to marriage breakdown. It may be that the behaviour arises from a lack of discretionary judgment, but it is unlikely that such a lack is so grave as to invalidate the consent of the person concerned.

An example of this might be selfishness with money because of a failure to understand the need to share finances. If the lack of sharing was not grave, this could be quite acceptable to both parties. Many people have grown up in families where father earned the money and gave a certain amount each week to mother for housekeeping. They may well expect to use that practice in their own marriages, but may not have realised that mother would often have asked father for a little more if the need arose. It happens that some breadwinners expect to give a set amount irrespective of how much they earn. In more extreme cases, he will have money for drink, cigarettes, a flutter on the horses and the pursuit of his hobbies, while she will have insufficient to buy necessary clothing. He might be so unrealistic that he fails to increase the amount to take account of inflation, or to recognise that new members of the family require feeding and clothing. These examples are more extreme, and the majority of breadwinners would be open to requests for additional finance.

> Margaret met Nelson and, after a two year courtship, they married. Both were earning an income before the marriage, and the expenses of their courtship were shared. They had agreed to put a certain amount each week into a joint building society account to save for a mortgage. Their one serious argument before the marriage occurred when Margaret discovered that Nelson had withdrawn his share of the money to buy camera equipment for his new hobby. She had fully forgiven him when he had promised to continue to make regular payments into the account without further withdrawals.

> After the wedding, they had retained their separate bank accounts at Nelson's insistence. It hadn't mattered initially, because they shared the bills and the mortgage payments. When Margaret became pregnant, she

decided she wanted to stop work for a few years in order to be able to give more time to their child. Nelson set up a standing order into her back account and insisted that she kept to that amount. Even when he was promoted, he refused to give her more on the grounds that he had earned the promotion so he had the right to say how the extra money was spent. Any decision regarding expenditure beyond that required from week to week became subject solely to Nelson's judgment of its necessity. He increased the standing order by a small amount when Oswald was born, but it was not enough, and Margaret had to resort to buying clothes for herself and Oswald from the second-hand shop. Meanwhile, Nelson could afford a leather jacket, a new car each year, and had enough left over to finance his regularly changing hobbies.

Margaret finally had to resort to taking a part-time job to make ends meet. When Nelson left her for another woman after Oswald's fourth birthday, she petitioned for a declaration of nullity of her marriage.

This is one of the more extreme examples of behaviour which might disturb a marriage. It is possible, even probable, that the Church could declare this marriage invalid because Nelson had failed to recognise the need to make a true gift of himself. It is an interesting example because, apart from the one instance when he withdrew money from their joint building society account, there was nothing to indicate that the marriage might not be happy. Furthermore, whilst it was his behaviour with money that was the principal problem in the marriage, it was his infidelity and desertion which brought it to an end.

Nelson's failure to recognise her needs and his selfish approach to money are indicative of a failure to evaluate the true nature of marriage. Other factors, such as his infidelity and abandonment of his family, might be totally irrelevant. It might, for example, have been the case that Margaret nagged him about his selfishness. No doubt his selfishness was destructive of their relationship, but her failure to recognise his inability to change could have driven them farther apart. On the other hand, she may have suffered in silence and, without his desertion, the marriage might have survived, albeit unhappily, for many years. As long as neither challenged it, the presumption of validity would hold.

Suppose that in this case Nelson had not been so selfish with money. Suppose that, while he insisted on separate bank accounts, he always gave money to Margaret whenever she asked; and she did ask freely. Furthermore, she had access to his bank statements and she knew how much he earned. It cannot readily be argued that he failed to make a gift of himself from the financial point of view, even though he insisted on separate accounts. On the face of it, the insistence on separate accounts is insignificant and there does appear to have been a genuine sharing of finances. Any investigation into the validity of the marriage would seek to understand Nelson's reasons for deserting Margaret and Oswald. If the marriage was seemingly happy until that time, the Church might respond to a petition for nullity with the answer that invalidity was not proved.

It can be seen, then, that the joining together of two people in marriage constitutes the joining together of all that those people are and have. Evaluation of the partnership which is to be established must necessarily include all that will be brought into that marriage.

In summary, if it can be shown that there was a failure to evaluate the marital decision, either in terms of the commitment involved or by reference to the circumstances of either party, and the marriage failed because of problems or difficulties which should have been foreseen, the marriage might be declared invalid.

The ground of lack of due discretion is a separate and distinct ground from that of inability, which is the subject matter of the next chapter. Nevertheless, as will be seen, there is considerable overlap between the two.

Hopefully, by now, the reader will be aware of the complexity of marriage nullity. The examples given in these chapters are by way of illustration only and the reader should be wary of drawing conclusions about specific marriages from them. Judgments about individual marriages should be left to the experts.

Chapter Twelve

Inability

A very simple principle has become the basis for a very important ground for nullity. The principle can be stated as "nobody is bound to the impossible". In other words, if a person cannot fulfil a promise, he can be said not to be bound by it.

A simple example will demonstrate the principle. Before you give me twenty million pounds to purchase Buckingham Palace from me, you are strongly advised to ensure that I possess the title to Buckingham Palace, and that I am able to pass it over to you. When I have disappeared with your money, you will have gained no better title to Buckingham Palace than you had previously. The contract will be invalid because it is impossible for me to pass over to you a title I do not possess.

Using similar reasoning, a marriage can be declared invalid if one of the parties is *unable* to assume one or more of the essential obligations of marriage. That is, if it can be shown that, at the time of the wedding, one party *could not* form that partnership of life and love which is marriage, the marriage will not have come into existence. To discover the nature of the essential obligations of marriage, it is necessary to return to the purposes of marriage, which are the well-being of the couple and the procreation and education of children.

Hence, it is obvious that the ability to have sexual intercourse is an essential element of the marital relationship, and not simply because intercourse is essential to the natural procreation of children. When intercourse is between two people who have made that gift of themselves to each other, it becomes a fundamental expression of the love of one spouse for the other. It is an act of love in its being fundamentally other centred; in other words, an act which, in its gift of self and acceptance of the gift of other, puts the well-being of the other before self-gratification. When this physical expression of the gift of self is not possible, there is the potential for declaring the marriage to be invalid.

Many Catholics believe that non-consummation of a marriage renders it invalid. This is not true, and the folly of such a notion is seen from the reality that the majority of marriages are not consummated for the first few hours or even days of their existence. The marriage comes into existence at the moment of consent, not the moment of consummation. However, it is possible that a non-consummated marriage might be rendered invalid because of the reason for the lack of consummation, using this ground of inability. The mere fact that it is not consummated does not prove invalidity. However, using special procedures, it is possible for the parties to a non-consummated marriage to remarry without obtaining a declaration of nullity. This is discussed more fully in Chapter 23.

When considering those who are unable to assume the essential obligations of marriage, the law adds an element which might appear at first sight to create problems. The law insists that the reason for the person being unable to assume the essential obligations of marriage must be founded in his or her psyche; that is, the inability must be for reasons of a psychological nature. Thus, this ground cannot be used in non-consummation cases if the reason for the inability to have intercourse is physical. However, if that was the case, the marriage could be declared invalid because of the presence of an impediment, provided that the problem was present at the time of the wedding.

If the problem was not present at the time of the wedding, the phrase "for better, for worse" can take on its full and possibly onerous meaning. If, for example, a man had an accident which rendered him permanently paralysed to the extent that full sexual relations were not possible, invalidity based on his inability would only be possible if the wedding took place after the accident. Assuming there is no other invalidating factor, should it happen that the wedding occurred before the accident, even just days before, the marriage would be valid.

The ground of inability is concerned with those who are unable to fulfil the obligations of marriage because of causes of a psychological nature. A potential difficulty arises in that it is not always possible to know that a failure by one party to live up to the marriage promises is due to an inability to do so rather than, for example, a failure to evaluate the nature of the marriage covenant. A person contemplating marriage should have considered his or her ability to fulfil the marriage promises before exchanging consent on the wedding day. Thus, it can be argued that a person who was unable to fulfil the essential obligations of marriage might also have been lacking due discretion of judgment by failing to evaluate that inability, if the inability should have been known before the marriage. Thus, in any genuine case of inability, it can usually be argued that the ground of lack of due discretion also applies.

Now consider the following example:

> Walter and Vicky married two years ago. In that time, they have only once come close to having intercourse. The problem is Vicky's reticence. She loves Walter dearly, but she is frightened of having intercourse with him. As a result of her fear, she becomes very tense in their love-making. The tension begins as soon as she anticipates penetration. The only time they almost succeeded was one time after she had had a little too much to drink at a party. She has even gone so far as to have a few drinks on occasion now to see if it will help, but to no avail. They have talked of seeking help, but agree that they would be too embarrassed talking about these matters to a doctor. Besides, they have argued, their love is sufficiently strong to overcome this difficulty.

> Initially they made love to the fullest extent they could, without intercourse. Each felt unfulfilled at the end, but neither expressed this to the other, both being careful to express satisfaction. Gradually, they stopped trying to make love, stopped talking about it, and stopped expressing their love physically. Walter was finally unfaithful and left Vicky to marry the other woman. He applied for a declaration of invalidity of his marriage to Vicky. When it came to asking her about the marriage, she confided that when she was younger she had been abused by an uncle, and it had been a very painful experience. She had never told anyone, not even Walter.

There would be little difficulty in declaring this marriage invalid. Vicky was quite simply unable to give herself to Walter in the way which marriage demands. Abuse of either party before marriage could result in that party being unable to give himself or herself in sexual intercourse. Counselling, together with patience, understanding and gentleness, can sometimes overcome a problem of this nature. Naturally, if Vicky could have been helped in that manner, she and Walter might have achieved a satisfactory sexual relationship, in time.

In theory, of course, if everyone adhered strictly to the moral code advocated by the Scriptures, most people entering marriage would be inexperienced in sexual matters when they married. As it takes time to develop other aspects of the relationship, so it takes time to develop the sexual side. Failure to consummate the marriage on the first night, or even within a few days or weeks, would not necessarily mean that the marriage is invalid. A temporary medical problem, for example, may mean that intercourse was unwise for a while. Embarrassment, initial tensions, fear of failure and general inexperience can lead to a very unsatisfactory sexual relationship in the early stages of marriage. Only if there is a lack of progress – no easing of embarrassment or tension, confidence waning rather than growing – might there be grounds for nullity.

Over time, the Church has come to accept that one single act of intercourse, although technically consummating a marriage, would not be sufficient to prevent a declaration of nullity. The psychological ability of each person must be the ability at the time of consent to make a gift of self over an extended period of time. Thus, it is to be expected that each couple would reach some acceptable level of sexual intimacy over a period of time. Failure to do so might indicate an inability to make an appropriate gift of self and so be the foundation for a plea of nullity.

Consider the following example:

> Yasmin and Zebedee married three years ago, but no longer have a sexual relationship. They had consummated their marriage, but Yasmin had found her experience of sexual intercourse with Zebedee to be painful and cold. He seemed unnecessarily rough and had no idea of her needs, seeming only to want his own satisfaction. She had tried to talk to him about it, but a combination of her awkwardness and his trivialisation of her complaint had resulted in no improvement. The frequency of intercourse had diminished as she made excuses to avoid his advances, and gradually the whole

of their relationship was affected. She simply could not bring herself to make love to him.

Should this marriage ever be challenged for nullity, the behaviour of each party would come under scrutiny. In that he only sought his own satisfaction, Zebedee could be said to have failed to make a gift of himself to Yasmin. His trivialisation of the matter is an important consideration when examining his ability. Perhaps he had a psychological block which prevented him approaching her complaint in a mature manner, or perhaps he simply did not see any need to make their love-making an act of giving, believing that if he was satisfied, she was too.

The fact that they were unable to achieve a satisfactory sexual relationship might be the foundation of a ground for nullity. However, Zebedee's failure to understand the self-giving nature of marriage within the sexual element of their relationship, and his failure to recognise the need to respond to her complaint, might also be important factors in a consideration of another ground – a possible lack in the adequacy of his discretionary judgment.

Because of the importance of the sexual relationship within marriage, there are many areas of concern when it comes to a consideration of validity. It is not just the absence of a sexual relationship which might be important. Any action which can be said to look more to self-gratification than to pleasing the other can be relevant when it comes to challenging the validity of a marriage. Such actions imply a lack of understanding of the self-giving nature of marriage, and hence lead to questions regarding the discretionary judgment of the person. This might occur, for example, when one party demands the use of unusual or unnatural practices.

The sexual relationship in marriage should be primarily an act of love, comprising a gift of self and embracing the well-being of the other. Various practices which have these as their end would not be invalidating. The Church would be more concerned about practices which gave pleasure to one spouse but were abhorrent to the other, or practices which strike at the very heart of marriage; for example, so-called wife-swapping. It will be clear that a practice which gives pleasure and joy to one couple might be totally abhorrent to another. It is only insofar as any practice seriously detracts from a particular marriage covenant that there might be implications for nullity.

This is as true for other aspects of marriage as for the sexual. There are implications for nullity when either party consistently acts in a manner which can be said to be contrary to the nature of marriage as a partnership seeking the well-being of each spouse.

> Aloysius and Bellissima have recently separated because she could take no more of his behaviour. Most of their friends and relatives are surprised at the separation. It is only those to whom Bellissima has confided who are relieved.
>
> For years she had seen two sides of Aloysius' character. In company he was charming and attentive to her and appeared the perfect husband and father. In private, however, things were very different.
>
> She had wanted to get away from home and had loved Aloysius sufficiently to put aside her doubts about marrying him. The doubts had arisen because he had struck her twice during the courtship. Each occasion had been when she had challenged him over very minor matters. She had decided to avoid such confrontations, but since shortly after the wedding he had been beating her regularly, always so that the bruises would not show. In private, she was a slave to him. In company, he would act the perfect husband. Bellissima finally left him when she became afraid of the effect his behaviour would have on their child.

It might be argued that Aloysius showed that he was quite capable of being the perfect husband and that, therefore, it is wrong to say that he was unable to assume the essential obligations of marriage. This argument would be unacceptable. Virtually everyone is capable of normal behaviour for a limited period of time. Marriage, by its very nature of a permanent institution, demands the ability to act over time in a manner which does not detract from its nature as a community of love. The fact that Aloysius simply did not act in that manner is considered sufficient proof that he could not do so.

The danger is in interpreting this principle too widely. It might be argued, for example, by the woman of an unfaithful husband that his infidelity amounted to acting in a manner which detracted from the true nature of their marriage. This could be true, but to prove invalidity on the ground that he was unable to assume the essential obligations of marriage, it would be necessary to show that his infidelity resulted from a personality disorder, and was not simply a moment of weakness or sin.

The conditions, known as nymphomania for women and satyriasis for men, which amount to an abnormally high sex drive, can effectively render a person unable to remain faithful in marriage. The existence of such a condition would normally be manifested by a history of infidelity with different partners. However, infidelity in marriage, even with several different partners, could be a sign of many different things, and the specific conditions of satyriasis and nymphomania can never be assumed. Besides the possibility that it might have been a moment of weakness or sin, infidelity could also be an indication of an unhappy marriage, of a selfish personality, or of ignorance of the nature of marriage. As an act which is contrary to the nature of marriage, the Church should always consider the implications of infidelity for the validity of the marriage, but these implications may well be irrelevant.

> Clarissa and Demetrius have been married for twenty-two years. The youngest of their four children has just left home, having found a job and her own flat. Their marriage was never wonderful, but they married freely and they did love one another. Over the years they had pursued their own interests, their mutual care and love for the children tending to be the only interest they had in common.

> For the last two years, Demetrius has been having an affair. Clarissa found out about it six months ago, but after her initial shock she realised how far apart she and Demetrius had drifted. They had discussed the situation at length, and Demetrius had told her he loved the other woman more than he loved Clarissa and he was not prepared to give her up. Clarissa was now resigned to the situation and asked only that Demetrius did all he could to avoid embarrassment to her and the children. They decided they would separate when the youngest left home.

The limited information available about this marriage would suggest that it is typical of many which fail after a number of years. Should either Demetrius or Clarissa ask for an investigation of the marriage for possible invalidity, it is likely that the Church would conclude that invalidity was not proved. This is an example where the infidelity of Demetrius was symptomatic of an unsatisfactory marriage rather than an incapacitating condition. No doubt it would have been preferable that he seek with Clarissa to renew their relationship, yet it is possible that neither was fully aware of the distance between them until it was too late.

Like many grounds for nullity, then, it is the facts of the marriage which determine if the ground of inability is appropriate in a particular case. Any personality disorder, which by definition is grounded in the psyche, can be invalidating if it results in a union which seriously undermines the well-being of either spouse or that of the children. The same is true of certain mental illnesses, dependencies (drink, drugs, etc.), or even a more temporary debilitating condition such as bereavement. The Church will examine each case on its merits, and it is obvious that the minor imperfections present in everyone's personality would not in themselves render a marriage invalid. There is always an important distinction to be made between circumstances which render a marriage invalid and those which simply render it difficult. The latter would not of themselves provide grounds for nullity.

Some problems in a marriage might not be invalidating in themselves, but might be manifestations of a disorder which is invalidating. A man who drinks heavily and who becomes dependent on drink during the marriage might well have started drinking as an escape from, say, the responsibilities of fatherhood. Since the procreation and education of children is one of the ends of marriage, a partner who is unable to accept the responsibilities of children could be judged unable to assume the essential obligations of marriage, providing that inability was the result of a problem existing at the time of the wedding. In this example, it would be the inability to accept the responsibilities of parenthood that would render the marriage invalid, rather than the drinking.

The variety and type of problems that could come under the umbrella of the ground of inability is virtually limitless. Furthermore, it would not be necessary for one problem in itself to be so severe as to present a consistent threat to a marriage. A combination of minor problems might have the same effect.

It is also apparent that the behaviour or personality of two people might make marriage between them impossible, while each would be capable of making a successful marriage with others. For example, two fiery tempered and stubborn individuals might find marriage to one another impossible, since the smallest argument would result in the complete breakdown of communication with little hope of reconciliation. Yet the marriage of one of these to a more placid and forgiving person might lead only to short-lived and soon forgotten arguments.

The use of this ground of inability in the marriage nullity process relies very much on the principle of "the proof of the pudding is in the eating". Whilst it can be very difficult to claim that one of the parties was unable to assume the essential obligations of marriage when that marriage had survived over an extended period of time, there is a need to discern the difference between a couple struggling with a successful union and a couple who have simply resorted to living together when the marriage has failed.

Before moving on to the next ground for nullity, it is interesting to note that there is an apparent anomaly between the use of this ground of inability and the Church's teaching on marriage. The Church teaches that the two ends or purposes of marriage, neither of which is presented as pre-eminent, are the well-being of the couple and the procreation and education of children. When a person enters marriage and consistently behaves in a manner which is detrimental to the well-being of the other, the marriage is capable of being declared invalid. However, the inability to conceive children, as opposed to the inability to have normal sexual relations, is not considered invalidating.

This is obviously right, since some couples are naturally unable to have children. In these marriages, it does not make sense to talk in terms of the two purposes of marriage. Hence, it might even be said that the one natural purpose of all marriages is to foster the well-being of the couple.

This would also appear to be reasonable in the light of the primary motive for people entering marriage. Whilst these can be many and varied, the desire to form a union with the chosen spouse would appear paramount. This desire is surely based on a belief that such a union will be mutually beneficial; that is, for the well-being of both. Children are not a certainty, and whilst procreation would be a natural and even desirable extension of the love of each spouse for the other, it is questionable that the desire to have children is as important to the couple as the desire to give themselves to each other for their mutual well-being. That having been said, for the time being at least, the Church continues to teach that marriage has two principal ends.

Chapter Thirteen

Error and Fraud

So far all the grounds that have been discussed under this heading of *defect of consent* concern those who are unable to give valid consent; because they lack the appropriate knowledge, have not properly evaluated the decision to marry, or because they lack the ability to put the marriage promises into practice. There are two other grounds which might also come under this general heading of those unable to give valid consent. They concern the areas of error and fraud. Although the scope for the use of these grounds is limited, they are occasionally cited as the grounds for declaring a marriage invalid.

There is an important distinction between error and fraud. Error comes from within the erring person when he has drawn an incorrect inference or conclusion from something, without there having been a deliberate act to mislead. Fraud occurs when a deliberate action is taken to ensure that an incorrect inference or conclusion is drawn by another person. Thus, I am in error if I marry a woman whom I believe to be rich, when she is in fact penniless. There is fraud attached only if she has taken steps to lead me to believe she is rich; or, knowing that I believe she is rich, she has made no attempt to correct me.

Error of person invalidates a marriage. If my intention is to marry Andrea, and the bride lifts her veil at the end of the ceremony to reveal Andrea's twin sister, the marriage can be declared invalid. I made a mistake by giving my consent to the wrong person. I can therefore claim that my consent was invalid. It is possible to think of other bizarre examples, but nullity is based on a simple matter of fact, and nothing further need be said about error of person.

Much more likely in reality, although still something of a rarity, is that the error concerns a quality of a person; that is, an error concerning some element of the person's character or physical being. The possibility of the marriage then being declared null depends upon whether or not that quality was directly and principally intended. This can be better understood by recognising that a quality which is directly and principally intended cannot really be distinguished from the person who has that quality, in the mind of the other. Thus, the quality is so important to the marrying partner that the marriage would not be taking place without it. In practice, the test here is the effect on the marriage of the truth being discovered. In other words, I cannot claim that a quality was directly and principally intended if, after discovering the quality did not exist, I nevertheless continued with the marriage.

Consider the following example:

> Earl was a doctor, and Frederica a nurse. They met when he came to work at the same hospital as she. She had always dreamed of marrying a doctor and, when it became obvious that there was a mutual attraction, they courted and married within a year. Two years later, Earl was called before the medical authorities to answer a charge of misconduct. During the course of the investigation, it was discovered that his qualification, which he had said was gained abroad, was false. When Frederica discovered this, she felt he had deceived her. More importantly for her, she had not in fact married a doctor. She could not bring herself to continue with the marriage, and left him.

Given these circumstances, it is possible that Frederica would be able to obtain a declaration of nullity of her marriage to Earl. She was in error in believing that Earl was a doctor, and it would appear that she principally and directly intended that the man she married would be a doctor.

However, in cases of this nature, the Church would want to be sure that the quality was principally and directly intended and that Frederica was not simply using this new knowledge as an excuse to depart from Earl; for example, because she was not particularly happy with him.

The range of possibilities for the use of this ground is, then, extensive. However, in practice, it is very difficult to show that a quality was so fundamental to the joining together of the couple that, without it, the marriage would not have taken place. Marriage is, after all, the joining together of two people, which is more than the joining together of two sets of qualities. It is for this reason that only the lack of a quality which is principally and directly intended will invalidate. Any other quality is incidental to the essence of the marriage.

The ground of fraud covers the same area as that of error. If the fraud is such as to secure the consent of the other, the marriage can be declared invalid, but only if the fraud was of such a nature that it could seriously disrupt the partnership of conjugal life.

It has, then, to be a grave fraud. It has to have been perpetrated to secure the consent of the other. If a man makes it known to his girlfriend that he is only willing to marry a virgin, and she hides from him the fact that she is not, he is entitled to claim invalidity. However, consider the following:

> Samantha and Titus have been courting for a few years and their wedding day is approaching. He has always thought that he would like to marry a virgin, and he has avoided full sexual relations until they are married. The thought has not crossed his mind that Samantha might not be a virgin, even though he knows that she has had at least one previous serious relationship.

> For her part, she has respected his stated wish to avoid full relations until they are married. She heard from his sister early in the relationship that he would prefer to marry a virgin. However, at that stage she felt it was too sensitive a subject for them to discuss the matter. By the time of the engagement, she had all but forgotten his sister's words.

> Some months after the wedding, Titus passes a comment regarding a friend who is marrying someone whom he knows to have had a previous sexual relationship, and says: "I'm glad I married a virgin." Samantha is taken aback, and tells him she wasn't. A big argument ensues, with Titus claiming that she deceived him, and Samantha denying it and stating that he knew she had had a previous boyfriend.

In these circumstances, a petition for nullity on the ground of fraud would almost certainly fail. Even if Titus' sister claims that Samantha knew he wanted to marry a virgin, it is not the case that Samantha deceived him in order to gain his consent to marriage. Furthermore, if it was so important to Titus that he marry a virgin, he would have been wise to have asked Samantha if she had had previous sexual relations.

Suppose that he had asked Samantha if she was a virgin, and she had replied affirmatively, knowing his desire to marry a virgin. Suppose also that, when he found out that she was not, it actually made little difference to their marriage. Here again, the claim of fraud would fail. It is true that there was some type of fraud but, since it was not so serious as to disrupt the partnership of conjugal life, it was also not serious enough to invalidate the marriage.

Thus it can be seen that the example of Earl and Frederica might well be error or fraud. Frederica intended only to marry a doctor, but she may not have mentioned it to Earl. She would naturally presume from seeing him in that role at work that he was what he claimed to be. If, however, she did say to Earl that she would only ever marry a doctor and he did not tell her the truth, she could claim that a fraud had been perpetrated against her.

Error and fraud can also give rise to circumstances which might be relevant to other grounds for nullity. For example, if I am determined to marry only a practising Christian, but do not question my intended spouse on this subject before marriage, it might be claimed that my discretionary judgment was lacking. Remember, however, that it takes a grave lack of discretionary judgment to invalidate a marriage (see Chapter 9).

The implications for other grounds are much more grave for fraud than for error. Any deception, but especially one so grave that it was intended to secure consent, is potentially damaging of the marital relationship, the good of which is very largely dependent on mutual trust. The discretionary judgment of anyone, therefore, who is prepared to deceive the other, must be in doubt, since it has grave implications for that person's understanding of marriage. Such deception can hardly be said to be compatible with the essential gift of self which marriage demands.

For the reasons just mentioned, fraud is the more serious of these two grounds in terms of its implications for the marriage covenant, and so the possibility of other grounds also being available for finding the marriage invalid. Nevertheless, if a successful plea of error of quality can be presented, there might also be reason to suspect the discretionary judgment of the erring person. Obviously, if a quality is so important that it cannot be separated from the person, the erring person would have done well to enquire about that quality before agreeing to marriage. A lack of such enquiry might lead one to wonder what other aspects of marriage were neglected in the period of evaluation before the marriage ceremony.

Chapter Fourteen

Defects of Intention

Another set of grounds for nullity arises from a defect in the intention of the parties. They may know the true nature of marriage and may have evaluated that nature with respect to the proposed partner, but it is also required that, at the time of giving consent, the intention of each was to enter marriage as envisaged by the Church.

The technical term for these defects of intention is "simulation". Those who simulate their consent are saying one thing with their lips, but intending another in their hearts. Simulation can be total; when one party goes through a marriage ceremony but does not intend to establish a marriage with the other. Alternatively, it can be partial; when marriage is intended, but some element, such as fidelity, children or permanence, is deliberately excluded.

> Imelda and Jeremiah have been courting for two years. Both are in their mid-twenties, and a common desire for marriage in principle led to an engagement just months after meeting.

> Initially they were very happy together, and expressed their feelings in a physical relationship. Both found this satisfactory, and felt this confirmed their decision to marry. Now Jeremiah is having doubts. He likes Imelda a lot, but the impending wedding – it is only four weeks away – has awakened him to the reality of the commitment he is about to make, and he is slowly recognising that, apart from a mutual enjoyment of a physical relationship, they have little in common,

> The problem is that everything is booked – the church, cars, photographer, reception, suits, flowers – and he knows that both sets of parents are looking forward to the day immensely. He cannot bring himself to tell anyone about his fears, and his refusal now to have

sexual relations with Imelda he excuses by saying he wants to wait until the honeymoon.

By the time the wedding arrived, Jeremiah was certain that he did not want to marry Imelda. He nevertheless acted out his role at the ceremony, and they left on honeymoon. It was a disaster. Jeremiah was distant all week, and at the end of that time they returned to their respective homes.

It is unfortunate that, fictional as this example is, it reflects an occasional reality. The advisability of calling off a wedding when one of the parties has severe doubts cannot be stressed enough.

When the problem is simply doubt, it can be argued that the process of evaluation is incomplete and the discretionary judgment of that party can be questioned. However, Jeremiah's certainty that he did not want the marriage means that he simulated his consent. At the ceremony, he said the appropriate words, but intended something quite different. His consent could therefore be declared invalid.

A more obvious case of simulation would occur when two people married simply so that one could acquire a new civilian status; for example, if a foreign student in Britain wished to stay at the end of his studies, but could not obtain an extension to his permit. By marrying a British national, he could obtain the right to remain in Britain. Of course, it is contrary to civil law to marry simply to gain nationality. Despite this, the Church would still require that a declaration of nullity be granted before either party could marry according to Catholic rites. Even though, on the surface, it is an obvious case of invalidity, the presumption of validity remains until the contrary is shown.

In any genuine case of total simulation, it would be expected that the couple did not live together as husband and wife for any period after the wedding. The Church would have difficulty in applying the ground to a marriage in which the couple had lived together for a few years. Nevertheless, the argument "we enjoyed living together, but never intended it to be permanent" might be sufficient to prove invalidity on the ground that the permanent aspect of marriage was excluded. This would be a case of partial simulation, rather than total simulation.

The ground most commonly encountered under the heading of partial simulation concerns the intention to exclude children from a marriage. A marriage in which one of the parties is determined not to have children is not a marriage as understood by the Church. Nevertheless, it is the case that many good marriages are naturally childless, and others do not result in children for many different reasons. Hence, great care is needed in interpreting the circumstances of each case.

> Karina and Luther married three years ago. As both were still young and keen to further their careers, they agreed to postpone having children for the foreseeable future, although both admitted that they saw children as part of their married life. Both have applied themselves to their careers and have been steadily promoted. Unfortunately, the marriage has suffered.

> Luther has been offered the opportunity of a good promotion two hundred miles away, and he wishes to take it. Karina, however, sees a move now as damaging her own prospects. They have decided that he will rent a flat near his work and return home at weekends. Their relationship suffers further.

> Karina now realises that the marriage is in jeopardy and decides that a child might help. Luther, however, sees the deterioration as having gone too far. Besides, he has met another woman at his work and is anxious not to be tied to Karina, given the current state of their relationship. He refuses to stop using contraceptives, which they have always used. When, six months later, the marriage fails, Karina asks the Church for a declaration of nullity on the ground that Luther had an intention against children at the time of the wedding.

It is likely that Karina's request on the stated ground would fail, although other grounds might well succeed given the materialistic attitude of this couple. She would no doubt wish to argue that Luther's stated intention to have children later in the marriage was proved a lie by his refusal to allow non-contraceptive intercourse, but it is unlikely that the Church would accept such reasoning. The other side of the argument is that Luther's refusal was simple common sense, given that their marriage was in such desperate straits at that time. Having children is rarely, if ever, the answer to an unhappy marriage. It could be argued that what was needed at that time was a fundamental reappraisal by the couple of what was important in their lives, and that perhaps there was a need to set the marriage on a firm foundation, if that was still possible, before thinking of children.

Compare the example of Karina and Luther with the following:

> Mary and Nikoli have been married for five years.
> Their pre-marriage discussions included the subject of
> children. Nikoli said he would prefer to wait a few
> years, whilst Mary was more keen. Nevertheless, she
> was doing well in her career and felt that a few years
> without children would give them a chance to get better
> established. Her comment that she would be prepared to
> wait three years was met by a non-committal response
> from Nikoli. Mary felt that in conscience she could not
> use contraceptives, but Nikoli insisted that he was not
> prepared to trust natural methods and he would use a
> condom.
>
> After three years, Mary started to drop hints that she
> would like to start a family. Nikoli argued, however,
> that they were not yet financially stable. He continued
> to use contraceptives. After Mary threw out his supplies
> one day, he simply withdrew before ejaculation.
> Arguments began and became so bad that the couple
> decided to separate. Mary eventually requested a
> declaration of nullity on the ground that Nikoli had an
> intention against children at the time of the wedding.

The important principle here is the exercise of rights. Marriage carries with it the natural right to sexual acts which are generative of children (in other words, non-contraceptive intercourse) and, insofar as that right can be said to be denied, the marriage covenant is not being fulfilled. (Out of this arose the argument that rape within marriage was not possible; a principle which the English civil law courts have recently found to be lacking in foundation. It seems clear that the exchange of rights on the wedding day does not impinge on the individual's right to respect and dignity.)

There are important distinctions to be made between the denial of the right to acts generative of children as exemplified by Luther (the former case), and that by Nikoli (the latter). Insofar as both women agreed with their husbands not to exercise that right for a few years, it cannot be argued that the right was denied to either of them. In the first example, Karina's right was denied at the end of her marriage, but this was a single incident of denial and was a result of Luther's perception of the state of their marriage at that time, rather than an expression of his intention at the time of the wedding. There is no certainty that Luther would have denied Karina her right if she had requested it earlier in the marriage.

In the second example, Mary chose not to exercise her right for the first three years of the marriage, so there was no question of Nikoli denying her that right. However, after that period, there was a sustained denial of Mary's right to acts generative of children.

In determining the exercise of rights in these cases, the Church has come to apply a simple rule. If it can be said that one party has reserved for himself or herself the right to say if and when a child would be conceived, it can safely be said that that person is denying the other the right which should be given in marriage. The right cannot be said to be denied if both parties agree not to have children, or if their marriage has been open to the possibility of children; that is, there have been periods of non-contraceptive intercourse when conception could have occurred.

Besides partial simulation, the denial of the right to sexual acts generative of children might in itself lead to the possibility of other grounds for nullity. A man who simply does not want the responsibility of fatherhood might have failed to make a proper evaluation of the nature of marriage. The same might be said of either party who saw the furtherance of a career, individual interests, or three foreign holidays a year as a higher priority than parenthood. Also, a woman who refuses to have children, because of the fear of the pain of childbirth, might be deemed unable to assume the essential obligations of marriage. This is not to say that a marriage involving any of these people could not turn out to be happy and apparently blessed by God. However, should any of them fail, there might be grounds for declaring such marriages to have been invalid.

Partial simulation can also be argued when one of the parties does not accept the permanent aspect of the marriage covenant. This would occur when one party reserved the right to end the marriage at will. Again, care is needed to distinguish a genuine intention at the time of the wedding to end the marriage at will, from the practical reality that divorce can be the most sensible thing after a failed marriage. Even the most ardent of Catholics may seek a civil divorce when their marriage has irretrievably broken down. Although there may be exceptions, this action at the end of the marriage cannot be said to have serious implications for the validity of the consent at the start of the marriage.

There would also be partial simulation if the element of fidelity in marriage was excluded from the consent of one of the parties. This would occur when the person was open to the possibility of having sexual relations with others if the opportunity arose.

Of course, it would be difficult to prove such an intention. An act of adultery is much more likely to occur because of a moment of weakness, perhaps when a marriage is having difficulties, than because one of the spouses considers fidelity in marriage to be unimportant. Nevertheless, a plea of intention against fidelity might be successful if it was shown that there was a continuing relationship with another partner at the time of the wedding (see the example of Albert and Priscilla on page 63), or that there was a pattern of regular infidelity throughout the marriage.

Again, another ground, rather than a defect of intention, might be more appropriate in an application for marriage nullity in which regular infidelity was alleged. Regular infidelity can be a sign of a poorly evaluated decision to marry or a personality disorder. In which cases, the grounds of lack of due discretion (Chapters 9–11) or inability (Chapter 12) would be more appropriate.

A final example of partial simulation could theoretically arise when one party intended to enter marriage, but seemingly did not intend to establish a community of life with his or her partner. Consider the following example:

> It was only weeks before the wedding that Othello was told by the company that they wanted him to go to South Africa for a month. The date of departure would be two days after his marriage to Petulla. He enjoyed his work and apologised to Petulla but made no attempt to avoid the trip, even though he knew that his company would have found a replacement if they had known of his circumstances.
>
> Shortly before his return to England, he telephoned Petulla with the news that he had been asked to stay in South Africa for another month. He lied to her when she asked if he had explained his situation to his employers. When his return was then delayed for a further three months, Petulla decided to act herself and wrote to the company to explain the situation and ask when they would allow her husband to come home. The company, not wanting to interfere in what they saw as a domestic matter, passed the letter over to Othello via his

immediate superior, who ascertained from Othello whether or not he would rather be back in the UK. Othello explained that he was quite happy where he was, doing the job for which he was paid. He and Petulla argued over the telephone, but he was adamant that he would not return home until his work in South Africa was finished. After a further twelve months, during which Petulla begged him to come home, she decided that it was time to seek a divorce. In her eyes, he was married to his work before her.

It does not seem unreasonable that a person getting married would have a right to expect the spouse to enter into a community of life in such a manner that a conjugal partnership can be formed. Hence, where one party apparently wills that he or she will live apart from the spouse without the consent of the other, the intention to form a community of life can be questioned.

However, even if this ground is not widely used, it would appear that Othello's perception of the meaning of marriage was lacking. In his case, discretionary judgment would demand an evaluation of the effect on the marriage of the request for him to go to South Africa. It would also be interesting to know: why he did not inform the company of his impending marriage, whether or not they discussed Petulla going out to live in South Africa with him, and why he continued to place a greater emphasis on his work than he did on his marriage. The answers to these questions would assist in ascertaining the correct grounds for an application for a decree of nullity.

Chapter Fifteen

Other Defects of Consent

This section would not be complete without an examination of the other possible grounds for nullity which can arise from a *defect of consent*. In practice, however, the number of cases in which they could be used successfully is extremely limited.

Marriage is an unreserved gift of self, and hence canon law makes special provisions when one or both parties attempts to impose conditions on the giving of consent.

A marriage cannot be validly contracted if there is a condition imposed concerning the future. Some possible examples of such a condition might be:

- "I will marry you only if you bear me a male heir."
- "I will marry you only if my mother can also live with us."
- "I will marry you only on condition that you never drink alcohol again."
- "I will marry you only on the condition that if the marriage fails you will be entitled to no more than £10,000 of my fortune."

It is, however, possible to enter marriage when the condition concerns the past or present. The following conditions could, therefore, be possible:

- "I will marry you only on condition that you are a millionairess."
- "I will marry you only on the condition that I am the father of the child you are carrying."
- "I will marry you only on the condition that you are not guilty of the crime with which you have been charged."
- "I will marry you only on the condition that you have never been married before."

- "I will marry you only on the condition that you are a virgin."

Note, the validity of the marriage depends on the condition being satisfied at the time of giving consent. Hence, it is irrelevant that the day after the wedding the millionairess loses half her fortune in a stock market crash. Providing she was a millionairess at the time of giving consent, the marriage is valid. If it was later shown that the condition was not satisfied at the time of the wedding, the marriage can be declared invalid. When it is not possible to verify the condition at the time of the marriage, the couple would be better waiting until such time as it was verified. However, this might present difficulties when, for example, the condition is dependent upon verifying the paternity of a child not yet born.

The final ground under the general heading of *defect of consent* concerns force and fear (there are others concerning marriage by proxy which will not be discussed in this book). This deals with those who see marriage as their only option when under the influence of some force or grave fear inflicted from outside, such as a threat of physical harm should the wedding not take place. It has to be distinguished from those who see marriage as the only option because of a set of circumstances, such as the girl being pregnant. The ground of force or fear would not apply in such circumstances, unless there was some outside force such as the girl's father threatening to kill the boy if he did not marry her. However, it suffices for the boy to believe that the father will kill him, even if the father would not actually do so.

It stands to reason that this ground is only applicable when one or both parties would not have entered marriage but for that force or grave fear.

> Angela and Barnabus met when they were both sixteen. They soon began a relationship; the first for each. They were very quickly besotted with one another, and became secretly engaged within weeks. On Angela's eighteenth birthday, they announced their intention to get married within the year.
>
> A month later, Angela met Reginald. He was two years older than she and obviously found her attractive. Over the next few months, Angela began to realise that she preferred Reginald to Barnabus. She began to have serious doubts about marrying Barnabus. After some thought, Angela told Barnabus that she was breaking off

their engagement, and she would not be marrying him the following month, as they had planned. Barnabus was furious. He told her that he loved her and that she was the only thing that made life worth living. Without her, he would kill himself. He told her that, unless she married him, he would throw himself under the wheels of a train.

Angela was too young and inexperienced to call his bluff. Furthermore, she did not feel that she could tell anyone about his threat. She agreed that she would marry him. Within months, she realised her mistake and sought to have the marriage declared invalid.

The ground of force and fear would be applicable here. However, other grounds would also apply. It is questionable whether Barnabus had a sufficient grasp of the meaning of the marital covenant if he was prepared to force Angela to take such action. Alternatively, and perhaps more likely, it might successfully be argued that Barnabus, perhaps through immaturity or self-centredness, was simply unable to make that gift of self which is demanded by marriage; that is, a gift which does not stifle the self-gift of the other.

Enough has now been said about the theory behind marriage nullity. The next few chapters explain how a declaration of nullity is gained in practice. There are a few other ways in which it is possible for some people, who have been a party to a wedding ceremony, to be able to enter another union. They will be examined in the final section of this book. However, first it must again be stressed that every case is unique, and readers should be wary of drawing definite conclusions about specific marriages from what is written here.

Section II

Chapter Sixteen
The Tribunal System

So far, reference to the word "tribunal" has been avoided. It is a word which conjures up many images in people's minds; images which might have deterred some from making an application for nullity. What is said in the next few chapters may assist in calming the fears of those who are put off by the name itself. The reality, however, is that an investigation into a marriage for possible invalidity is carried out by the diocesan tribunal.

Marriages are examined for invalidity using one of two processes: the documentary process, or the formal process. The documentary process is generally used for marriages which are invalid by reason of a defect of form or because of the presence of an impediment. As its name suggests, invalidity is proved by simply producing the relevant documents to show, for example, that one of the parties to a register office wedding was a Catholic. Similarly, many impediments can be proved by simply producing documents.

Cases which cannot be proved using the documentary process (and this would include all cases of invalid consent) would be subjected to the formal process. The bulk of the work of diocesan tribunals is the examination of failed marriages using the formal process. Before proceeding to an explanation of the workings of the formal process, it is useful to have some idea of the tribunal system as a whole.

Each diocese can have its own tribunal. The tribunal is headed by the diocesan bishop. However, canon law, recognising that most bishops will have more than enough work to do, requires the bishop to appoint a priest to officiate over the tribunal. His title is "Officialis" or "Judicial Vicar". A vicar is one who is delegated to act in the name of another. Hence, the judicial vicar is delegated by the bishop to act with the bishop's judicial power. The tribunal will also normally have a number of other personnel appointed to various roles, about which more will be said later.

The function of the tribunal is usually defined by the diocesan bishop, and it can be asked to judge on any matters of contention within the diocese. However, in practice it is rare for a tribunal to hear any case other than applications for nullity of marriage. For this reason, many diocesan tribunals have become known simply as "marriage tribunals".

Some dioceses do not have a sufficient number of qualified personnel or other resources to establish their own tribunals. In these cases, two or more dioceses may share a tribunal, and these are known as inter-diocesan or regional tribunals. Whereas most dioceses in England and Wales now have their own tribunals, the whole of Scotland is served by one tribunal, known as the Scottish National Tribunal, based near Glasgow. Ireland is served by four regional tribunals, no diocese having its own.

Besides these tribunals, the role of which is to hear cases in first instance, there is also a system of appeal tribunals (also known as tribunals of second instance). These are tribunals which are designated by the authorities in Rome to hear appeals against the decisions of the first instance tribunals. In England and Wales, the tribunals of the Westminster, Liverpool, Southwark, Birmingham, and Cardiff Archdioceses and the Wrexham Diocese have been appointed as appeal tribunals. In Ireland, the National Appeal Tribunal of Ireland, based in Dublin, hears appeals from the regional tribunals. All appeals from the Scottish National Tribunal are heard in Birmingham.

No tribunal may hear its own appeals. The result is that Birmingham appeals are heard in Liverpool, Liverpool appeals heard in Westminster, and Westminster appeals heard in Birmingham. Southwark has a separate first and second instance tribunal, and appeals from one are heard in the other. Cardiff appeals are heard in Wrexham, and Wrexham appeals in Cardiff. An appeal tribunal has been appointed for every English and Welsh diocese, usually along provincial lines where this is practicable. So, for example, the Liverpool Tribunal hears appeals from the tribunals of the Lancaster, Salford, Hexham and Newcastle, Hallam, Leeds and Middlesbrough dioceses, as well as those of the Birmingham Archdiocese.

Besides this second level of tribunals, there is the Roman Rota. This is the usual third instance tribunal, and it hears appeals from appeal tribunals. However, the Rota can also hear any case, from anywhere in the world, in first, second or third instance. Finally, certain cases, such as those involving Heads of State, are specifically reserved to the Holy Father. The purpose of this is to attempt to ensure that local tribunals can act without any undue influence from civil powers. This may appear to be granting special privileges to the rich and famous, but in fact the Rota is likely to take longer to complete the application than many local tribunals.

Applications for nullity using the formal process are not granted after only one hearing. More details about this will be given later (Chapter 21). For now, it suffices to say that two tribunals must declare a marriage invalid before a declaration of nullity is granted.

The first step in any application for nullity is for one of the parties of the marriage to apply to the local marriage tribunal (a list of the addresses of the tribunals of Great Britain and Ireland is given in appendix 1). However, it is possible that the local tribunal will not be able to hear the case because it lacks competence.

The question of competence means that not every tribunal can hear any application for nullity. A tribunal which hears a case when it is not competent is effectively wasting its time. Canon law renders invalid the judgments of non-competent tribunals. Hence, a tribunal receiving an application for nullity will begin by considering whether or not it is competent. If it is not, it should refer the case to a tribunal which is competent.

The tribunals competent to hear marriage cases are either the tribunal of the place where the marriage was celebrated, or the tribunal (it may be the same one) of the place where the other party to the marriage has a domicile, which is usually the permanent address. In some circumstances, it is possible for the tribunal of the domicile of the applicant to hear the case, or the tribunal of the place where most of the evidence is to be collected.

> Arthur's marriage to Beauty has ended in divorce. They married in Liverpool, but shortly afterwards moved to Northampton. After they separated, Arthur moved to Birmingham. His family live in and around Lancaster. Hers live around North London.

If Arthur wished to apply for a decree of nullity, he could approach one of the following tribunals:

> Liverpool – being the place of marriage,
> Northampton – being the place where Beauty has a domicile,
> Birmingham – being the place where he himself has a domicile, providing the Officialis in Northampton did not object,
> Lancaster or Westminster – whichever is the diocese in which most of the witnesses live, and the likely place where most of the evidence will be collected, providing the Officialis in Northampton did not object.

If Beauty wished to apply for a decree of nullity, she could approach the following tribunals:

> Liverpool – being the place of marriage,
> Birmingham – being the place where Arthur has a domicile.
> Northampton – being the place where she has a domicile, providing the Officialis in Birmingham did not object.
> Westminster or Lancaster – whichever is the diocese in which most of the witnesses live, and the likely place where most of the evidence will be collected, providing the Officialis in Birmingham did not object.

It is normal practice for one of the first two named tribunals to hear the case.

Finally, a word of comfort for those put off by the title itself. The parties are never asked to present themselves before a panel of tribunal personnel, or to attend a formal hearing of the case. Nor is the purpose of the tribunal to make moral judgments on anyone. It appears that some people are put off by the thought of having to admit that they have remarried, that they were unfaithful in the marriage, or that they have done similar acts which are against official Church teaching. Tribunal personnel are well used to hearing such statements, and it is not their function to make moral judgments.

Most applicants will find that one or two visits to the tribunal offices is all that is required, and then they will normally only be seen by one person for an interview. Occasionally it is possible for an applicant to obtain a declaration of nullity without having had to attend the tribunal offices at all.

Chapter Seventeen
The Petitioner

The person making the application for nullity is known as the petitioner, or the plaintiff. In theory, the application begins by the person presenting a petition to the diocesan bishop asking for an investigation into the validity of the marriage. In practice, however, very few petitioners make contact with the tribunal in this way. Most are put in touch with the tribunal via a third party, such as a parish priest.

Any person, whether Catholic or non-Catholic, can petition for a declaration of nullity of his or her marriage as long as the other party is still alive. The most common reason for an application is that the petitioner wants to remarry, or has already married in a register office and wants the union recognised by the Church. The second most common reason seems to be that the petitioner wants to gain some peace of mind from a successful application.

Tribunals are usually interested in the reason for a petitioner seeking to have the marriage declared null, but the motive would not normally affect the progress of a case. It has, however, been known for tribunals to reject cases which do not appear to be adequately motivated. For example, an application from a non-Catholic, formerly married to a non-Catholic, and now wishing to marry a non-Catholic, might result in the tribunal deciding that, since a declaration of nullity would have no practical effect on any of the parties concerned, it would not hear the case.

The first duty of the tribunal is to safeguard the sacrament of marriage by ensuring that, if there is any hope of success, the couple are given every opportunity to resume their married life. This does not mean that tribunals will try to persuade a couple to reconcile, but it does place an onus on the tribunal staff to ensure that there is no hope of reconciliation before investigating the marriage for invalidity. No good will be served if a declaration of nullity is issued only for the couple to decide that they wish to remain together. Most tribunals will assume that if a couple have obtained a civil divorce, then any chance of reconciliation has passed. This is one reason why most tribunals ask that the couple obtain a civil divorce before proceeding with an application for nullity.

There is a much more practical reason for tribunals insisting that a civil divorce is obtained. That is to protect tribunal personnel from being subpoenaed by the civil courts to attend civil divorce proceedings. The civil courts would have the right, in civil law, to demand that evidence given in an application for nullity be made available for the divorce hearing. This would not only place the tribunal personnel in an impossible position, but would also act as a deterrent against people thinking of applying for nullity. It is clearly advantageous, then, to have the civil divorce proceedings completed before an application for nullity is made.

Each individual tribunal has its own preferred method of beginning the nullity process. Some will require a few written details from the petitioner before requesting an interview. Others will simply ask the petitioner to attend for a preliminary interview, and later for a more detailed interview. Some may proceed directly to a full interview. Arrangements can often be made for the petitioner to be interviewed by his or her parish priest, or by some other suitably trained person in the locality. Potential applicants should contact their local tribunal for more information about its particular procedures.

Since the majority of applicants would require guidance in drawing up a petition, most tribunals undertake this task for them using the results of the first interview. Once it has been read and any necessary amendments have been made, the applicant will sign the petition. A typical petition might read as follows:

18 Main Street,
Any Town,
Somewhere.

My Lord Bishop,

I, Mary Margaret Marie Murphy, married John Joshua James Jones on 18th September 1961 at the church of All Saints, Any Town. I was eighteen at the time and he was twenty-three. We are both Catholics. We separated in January 1963, and were divorced five years later.

We courted for only seven months before I got pregnant. We were in love and had thought about marrying, but not so soon. The wedding was quickly arranged and within three weeks we were married.

We lived with my parents until the baby was born in February 1962, when we got a council house. After that, John would never stay in. He refused to help me with the baby and was not giving me enough money. The bills were unpaid because all his money went on drink and the horses, and I had to ask my Dad for help. John continually arrived home drunk and I finally asked him to choose between me and his current lifestyle. He changed for a week, but was then back to drinking every night. I decided to return to my mother's with the baby in January 1963.

In 1970, 1 met a single man and we married in the register office in 1973. I long to return to the full practice of my faith. Therefore, I am writing to request an investigation into my marriage to John Joshua James Jones for possible invalidity in canon law.

signed: Mary Margaret Marie Smith
(née Murphy)

14th April 1982

The petition is usually addressed to the bishop as official head of the tribunal, although in practice he will rarely see it. It gives a brief outline of the marriage, the names of the parties, the place of marriage and the important dates. As its name suggests, it is a petition for an investigation into the validity of the marriage. (Guidance to writing a petition is given in appendix 2).

Theoretically, the petition should state the grounds upon which the request is based. However, in practice only a trained canon lawyer will accurately assess the possible grounds for nullity, and it is unrealistic to expect petitioners to be able to state the grounds upon which the application will be based. To produce a petition like that above would be possible for most people, though not everyone.

In theory, before a petition is accepted for hearing, the grounds must be decided and agreed upon by the parties. Again, in marriage nullity cases, that is not always practicable. It assumes that people understand the grounds and that the parties have been able to present an objective and detailed picture of the marriage. In practice, the best grounds upon which to base an application will not be clear until all the evidence is collected. It is in nobody's interest for tribunals to assess cases on grounds which will not succeed. An ability to change the grounds at any time, in order for each case to be argued using those grounds most likely to succeed, best serves the needs of all concerned. In the event that a marriage is not declared invalid by one tribunal, the appeal tribunal can always introduce new grounds if it feels they are appropriate and have a chance of success.

This process of selecting grounds would appear at first sight to favour an application for nullity. "If we can't get a decree of nullity on one ground, let's try another until we find one that works." It has to be remembered that the odds are stacked against any particular marriage being declared invalid. It is only broken marriages that are tested for nullity, and only a small proportion of those would come before a tribunal. Even then, there is no guarantee of success. It should also be remembered that a marriage, although presumed valid, either is or is not valid from the moment of giving consent on the wedding day. The role of the tribunal is to discover the truth of that situation. There is no sense in which the tribunal's role is to look for excuses to declare a marriage invalid. However, justice demands that if a marriage is invalid, the tribunal seeks to declare that fact.

The presentation of the petition is the first stage of an application and forms the basis of the first decision to be made by the tribunal. At this stage, the tribunal can accept or reject the petition. As already stated, there is nothing to be gained by the tribunal processing applications which have no chance of success. It is a waste of the tribunal's resources and can give false hope to the petitioner. The tribunal can, therefore, reject an application from the beginning.

It is possible for tribunals to be too quick to reject petitions. A petition alone is inadequate as a basis for assessing the viability of an application for nullity. It is unlikely to do justice to all the relevant circumstances of a marriage and its breakdown.

Even when a petition has been drawn up from a detailed interview, it is not unknown for witnesses (see Chapter 19) to provide a much greater understanding of the problems in a marriage than has the petitioner. Many petitioners are simply unable to be objective, both about the reasons for the marriage failing and their own deficiencies, while the other party might be blamed for faults which, it transpires, have been exaggerated out of all proportion.

For this reason, not only will tribunals be careful about rejecting petitions, but parish priests and others who advise potential applicants before they approach the tribunal should be wary of commenting on the chances, either positively or negatively, which an applicant might have in presenting a petition for nullity. It is not unknown for people to have been put off applying for a declaration of nullity by a well-meaning parish priest, only later to have had the marriage declared invalid when the applicant has approached the tribunal by a different route. It is worth remembering that, whilst all priests will have studied some canon law during their priestly training, few are trained to the depth necessary to make sound judgments on the validity or otherwise of a marriage. It is the tribunal judges who ultimately decide the matter on the evidence before them, and any other person's opinion about the validity of the marriage will not be taken into consideration.

When a petition for an investigation into the validity of a marriage is rejected by the tribunal, the petitioner has a right of appeal against that decision. A simple request for an appeal against the tribunal's decision is enough. The tribunal should then forward all the relevant documents to its appeal tribunal. The appeal tribunal's role, on this occasion, is simply either to confirm the rejection or to instruct the first instance tribunal that the petition is to be accepted. However, even if the appeal tribunal upholds the decision at first instance, there is really no reason why a petitioner might not present a new petition in the future.

At this stage – the acceptance or rejection of a petition – the tribunal is only making a judgment about the viability of an application. The tribunal should reject a petition only when it appears that the case has no chance of reaching a successful conclusion. Besides the danger that the petition will not do justice to the facts, even a full interview with the petitioner is not guaranteed to present the truth. The right to reject petitions is always going to present hard-pressed tribunals with the dilemma of finding the right balance between obtaining quick justice for those whose marriages should be declared invalid and processing cases which will not result in a decree of nullity being granted. Less hard-pressed tribunals can afford to err on the side of caution and hear every case which might have a chance of success.

> After fifteen years of married life, Maria's husband left her. He told her that he no longer loved her and had found somebody else. That was five years ago, and Maria fell in love last year and wants to marry the new man in her life. She has, therefore, approached her local tribunal and has given formal evidence. She reports that her courtship with her husband was normal and seemed happy enough. They were both in their early twenties when they married. The greatest sadness of their marriage was that they had had no children, but they seemed to be happy as a couple despite that.
>
> They had never sought to discover the reason for their lack of success in bringing children into the world. It was only in the last couple of years that they seemed to drift apart. Her husband had been socialising more without her, but still only once or twice a month. She had never suspected he had another woman until he told her just before his departure. He had been unable to tell her why he found the need for somebody else. She assumed he just didn't find her physically attractive, as sexual relations, which had always been infrequent, had ceased altogether in the last few years.
>
> On the basis of this information, the tribunal rejected her petition. When she appealed, the appeal tribunal asked for the husband to be interviewed before it made its decision about a full hearing. Maria's husband agreed to be interviewed on the condition that his evidence would not be revealed to her. The tribunal agreed to his condition with the reservation that, if he made allegations about Maria, it retained the right to put them to her.
>
> When the husband was interviewed, he revealed that he did not in fact have another woman, but had finally come to acknowledge to himself that he was homosexually orientated. For many years he had feared that he might be. Only when he had finally come to accept it did he decide that he could no longer continue to live the lie of acting the role of being a husband to Maria. The appeal tribunal instructed that the case should be heard, and Maria's application was ultimately granted.

This is an example of the danger of prematurely rejecting petitions. In an ideal situation, and because of the complexity of human relationships, tribunals would hear all applications for nullity. This would not only reduce the risk of invalid marriages being rejected at the petition stage, but it would also help petitioners to feel that the Church had given them a fair hearing.

In theory, when a petition has been accepted, the petitioner should then be fully interviewed. In practice, as has been said, many petitioners will be interviewed before a petition is drawn up.

The most important evidence obtained in any application for nullity is usually that of the petitioner. It is obtained during an extensive interview in which the petitioner, in response to a series of questions, is asked to talk about the marriage and its breakdown. However, marriage is a relationship of two people and there is more that is relevant to the approach of each to the marriage than just the time they spent together as a married couple. Consequently, the interviewer will also ask for details of the backgrounds of the parties, their courtship, their motives for marriage and their personalities, as well as requesting a history of the marriage and the reasons for its failure. Unfortunately, it is sometimes necessary for these questions to be intrusive, but the tribunal will always take steps to safeguard statements made in confidence.

The results of this interview will form the major part of the petitioner's evidence. Most of the evidence is collected in this way, and only written evidence is presented to the judges at the time of the hearing.

The tribunal is searching for truth. Only if it is reasonably certain that the truth has been discovered can it make a judgment on a particular marriage. It is for this reason that petitioners are encouraged to be fully open about themselves, the marriage and its problems. It is also for this reason that others besides the petitioner are asked to give evidence.

It is appropriate to give a few words of advice for anyone who is thinking of making an application for nullity of marriage, or perhaps is already in the process of doing so. Following this advice will also assist the tribunal in the handling of the case.

DO

- Ask the tribunal staff if you want any information about the procedure.

- Request a progress report if you have not heard anything for a while. This is particularly important if you think you should have heard from the tribunal. (However, remember that the procedure takes many months and even years to complete. Please be patient if you have been advised to wait.)
- Answer letters promptly.
- Tell the whole truth. There is almost certainly nothing you can say which will not have been heard before by the tribunal staff.
- Assist the tribunal, and hence others who may wish to apply, by paying whatever you can towards the costs incurred.
- Inform the tribunal if, for any reason, you decide not to proceed with your application. The papers already collected will normally be filed away in case you should change your mind at a later date.

DON'T
- Tell others what to say when they give evidence. It could *seriously* jeopardise your chances of success.
- Be afraid to approach the tribunal about taking up a case which has lapsed.
- Expect tribunal staff or anyone else to tell you your application will succeed. There can be no certainty until a declaration of nullity is handed down and, no matter how promising your application may appear, tribunal staff will not be able to promise anything.

Chapter Eighteen
The Respondent

Amongst the questions put to the petitioner at the time of the interview, if not before, will be some concerning the former spouse, who is known throughout the process as the respondent. It is an unfortunate title, because it seems to imply the need to respond to allegations made by the petitioner. It should always be remembered that the petition is for an investigation into the marriage and not into the behaviour of either party. It is the presumption of validity of the marriage which is attacked, not the respondent. It is perhaps useful to remember that grounds can be found in either the petitioner or the respondent or both, but the judgment concerns the validity of the marriage.

Unless there are children involved to whom both parties have access, it is unlikely that the couple will remain in contact. Often, particularly if the divorce has been acrimonious, the idea of involving the other party might seem quite repugnant to a petitioner.

The tribunal has a duty to inform the respondent that a petition for nullity has been presented; after all, the results of the hearing will affect both parties. Furthermore, the respondent has a right to take part in the proceedings, in the same way as the petitioner. However, at no time need the petitioner and respondent meet or communicate with one another, nor will the tribunal pass on the address of the petitioner to the respondent. What is required of the petitioner is that all reasonable efforts are made to provide the tribunal with an address at which the respondent can be contacted. The tribunal will do the rest.

The requirement that the respondent be informed of the application for nullity is considered of the utmost importance. Hence, the petitioner is required to make some considerable efforts to find a current address for the former spouse. If the address of the spouse cannot be found, the tribunal will often settle for the address of a relative of the respondent, on the assumption that the relative will be able to forward any letters. It is only in extreme circumstances, and when the tribunal is satisfied that the petitioner has made reasonable efforts, that a case will proceed without the respondent having been contacted directly.

Having said that, the important point is that respondents be given their rights, not that they exercise those rights. Even though invited to take part, many respondents choose not to do so, often simply ignoring the invitation. Of those who do reply, few actually choose to co-operate by providing information. Only a small proportion agree to be interviewed in the same manner as the petitioner.

Since the tribunal is seeking the objective truth of the matter, which it would be very difficult for one party alone to give, some evidence from the respondent is to be recommended. To encourage respondents to give information when they might be unwilling to be interviewed, they are often given the option of answering questions through the post. This increases the chance of obtaining some information, although it can restrict the value of the evidence obtained.

A letter from the tribunal informing a respondent that a former spouse is applying for nullity sometimes seems to provoke an adverse reaction. Some respondents claim they do not believe that marriages can be declared invalid. Others claim it seems too much like raking up the past. To some, it feels like a personal attack. To others, it seems too much of a personal matter to be subjected to the scrutiny of outsiders. Some just see the whole process as irrelevant and unnecessary, and wonder why their former spouses cannot simply remarry without involving them. For any one or several of these reasons, respondents will frequently decline to take part and even be quite angry. A respondent might object to the fact of an application, but he or she cannot prevent the investigation taking place. Equally, if a respondent co-operates and the petitioner then requests that the case be abandoned, the respondent can ask for the process to be completed.

The evidence of the respondent can enhance the likelihood of the tribunal being sure that the truth of the matter has been revealed. Because individuals can only describe events in the light of their own thoughts and observations, the story of the marriage as told by a petitioner will always be subjective. Evidence from the respondent will usually present a different picture of the same story. If there are significant discrepancies between the two depositions, such as accusations of infidelity which are denied by the other, the tribunal will seek clarification before proceeding to the next stage of the process.

On a purely practical note, tribunals will often suggest that the petitioner write to the respondent to tell him or her about the application for nullity. When the reason for the request is explained to the respondent by the petitioner, the tribunal's letter, which informs the respondent of the application and invites him or her to take part, will not come as a surprise and the respondent may be more willing to co-operate. However, it is appreciated that not all petitioners would want to have that contact with the former spouse.

It might be thought that the rights of the respondent were being ignored if he or she objected to an application for nullity but the case was nevertheless heard. This is not so. Both parties have the right to submit a petition, and the petitioner is the party whose petition is first accepted. Neither party receives preferential treatment. The respondent, like the petitioner, has the right to name witnesses and have legal representation.

When a respondent does object to the proceedings, the tribunal will take note of the objections, but will still proceed if it believes there are grounds to do so; namely, that there appears to be a chance of a nullity being granted. A declaration of nullity is, after all, only a recognition in law that a marriage is invalid and has been since the wedding day. Thus, it is a search for truth, and justice might be thwarted if one party had the right to call a halt to the proceedings without the consent of the other.

Chapter Nineteen

Witnesses and Other Proofs

In order to declare a marriage invalid, the tribunal needs to be sure of two things: that the truth of the matter has been discovered (that is, that the relevant facts have been established), and that those facts amount to an invalid marriage. Hence, the tribunal cannot simply rely upon the story as told by the petitioner. The judges need to have some certainty that the story he or she has presented is the objective truth as distinct from the truth as perceived by the petitioner.

Evidence from the respondent might well help them to reach that certainty, but it is also possible that conflicts between the evidence of the parties will leave the tribunal confused about where the truth lies. Evidence from witnesses is helpful, both in corroborating the story of the parties and in providing a more objective picture of the marriage.

Both parties can name witnesses, and the petitioner is expected to name a few. The number of witnesses requested varies from tribunal to tribunal. Some tribunals ask the parties to name just two or three, whilst others will ask for six. It is not the quantity so much as the quality of the evidence of witnesses which is important. The evidence of two or three good witnesses is usually quite adequate. Those tribunals which ask for more are usually erring on the side of caution.

Witnesses can be anyone, of any religion or none, with knowledge of the parties and their marriage. The most obvious witnesses are the parents of the parties and any brothers or sisters. Close friends to whom the parties have confided can also be very useful. Since it is the time of the wedding which is ultimately important – it was at that moment that the marriage either did or did not come into existence – it is clearly preferable that witnesses knew the couple at that time. However, other witnesses can prove useful, and should not simply be dismissed out of hand.

Before naming witnesses, the parties are asked to ensure that they are willing to act in that capacity. Most family members and friends are usually only too happy to help. As with the petitioner, the evidence of witnesses is gathered by means of an interview. Again, different tribunals have different procedures. Some insist that witnesses come to the tribunal office for interview, while others arrange for witnesses to be interviewed in their own homes, or perhaps a local presbytery.

Sometimes a tape is used to record the witness's evidence, and this is later transcribed onto paper. More often the interviewer will make a written record of the answers. At the end of the interview the recorded answers are read back to the witness, who can ask for any amendments to be made. The witness then signs the record of the interview as a proof of authenticity. If the interview has been taped, a separate document is required for this purpose. Witnesses are generally asked to give their evidence under oath.

Witnesses often seem concerned about what they will have to say. In fact, they can only say what they know, and nothing more is required than that they tell the truth as they perceived it. In order to ensure that witnesses reveal as much as they know, a standard questionnaire, usually with a few modifications for the particular case, will be used for the interview. The questions tend to be very wide ranging, covering such areas as the behaviour of the parties, their personalities, events before the marriage, events during the marriage, and the reasons for the breakdown, amongst others.

Witnesses are encouraged to give full evidence. They are requested to state opinions and hearsay evidence, as well as facts they have learned for themselves. It is up to the judges to give appropriate weight to the evidence collected. Nowadays, many tribunals have trained volunteer lay people in the role of auditor. It is the auditor's role to record the witness's testimony and present it to the tribunal.

Besides witnesses to the marriage, so-called "expert" witnesses can also be called. If, for example, a woman is claiming that she was consistently beaten and needed medical attention, it would normally be possible to obtain medical records from her doctor. Similarly, when mental illness is alleged. Naturally, the tribunal can only obtain this evidence with the co-operation of the person concerned.

Sometimes tribunals will ask for a psychiatric report on a case. The role of the psychiatrist will be to report on the personalities of the parties, insofar as this can be ascertained from the written evidence available, or to give guidance on the nature of a particular disorder or illness.

It can happen that petitioners are not able to find the appropriate number of witnesses, or that the evidence available from the witnesses does not provide sufficient corroboration of the petitioner's story. It is sometimes possible, in such cases, to obtain character witnesses; that is, people who have no knowledge of the marriage, but who can attest to the truthfulness of one or both parties.

Petitioners approach the tribunal on matters of conscience. They wish to remarry or have already done so, and would feel guilty without a declaration of nullity. In such cases, nothing is to be gained by telling lies. Some comfort can be gained from this, but tribunals will be wary when the reason for seeking a nullity is not one of conscience. Petitioners should also bear in mind that applications for nullity have been known to fail because the judges did not think the truth had been forthcoming.

It is difficult to set guidelines as to the sufficiency of the evidence required by tribunals. Whereas canon law puts the onus on the petitioner to prove the invalidity of the marriage, equity demands that tribunals assist petitioners in this matter. Until such time as the case is brought to definitive judgment, it is never too late to admit further evidence. Nevertheless, in theory, at least, and to expedite matters, the tribunal will pronounce a time after which further evidence will not be admitted.

Chapter Twenty

Concluding the Process

There are roughly five stages involved in examining a marriage for possible invalidity using the formal process: the presentation and acceptance of the petition, the collection of the evidence, the presentation of arguments for and against nullity, the judgment, and the appeal. The first two of these formed the subject matter of earlier chapters. This chapter explains the third and fourth stages of the process, and the roles played by the various tribunal personnel.

When all the evidence has been collected, the advocate presents the arguments in favour of nullity. An advocate who feels that further evidence would be appropriate may suggest that it be collected. Furthermore, if other grounds could appropriately be introduced, now is the time to have them included. The advocate's role is, therefore, to ensure that the best case is made for declaring the marriage invalid. Justice is not served by cases being pronounced unproved when evidence of invalidity is available but not collected, or the wrong grounds have been proposed.

When the advocate has presented written reasons for declaring the marriage invalid, the defender of the bond will examine the case and present those arguments, again in writing, which the judges ought to consider against the marriage being declared invalid. It is surprising to find in canon law that, while all cases must be passed to a defender of the bond for comment before the judges give their verdict, the use of an advocate is not obligatory. In cases when an advocate is not used, the defender of the bond and the judges have a special duty in conscience to ensure that justice is not thwarted by the absence of advocate's pleadings.

Canon law demands that the defender presents only those reasonable arguments which suggest the bond of the marriage should be preserved. It is not expected that the bond be defended at all costs, and there is again a risk of thwarting justice if the judges are misled by clever but false arguments. If the defender can find no reasonable arguments to present to the judges – that is, the case is very obviously proved – this should simply be stated.

The defender also has a role much earlier in the process, including the right to be present at any interview to ensure that it is being conducted fairly. The defender may also direct that additional questions be asked of the parties or their witnesses in order to clarify the evidence.

The advocate acts before the defender of the bond. Thus, when writing his arguments, the defender can point out the weaknesses in the advocate's arguments, as well as more general weaknesses in the evidence and the facts. To redress this advantage in favour of the bond, the advocate will be given the opportunity to reply to the comments of the defender, who will then be given the chance of making further observations. When both advocate and defender are satisfied, the case will go to the judges.

The arguments presented by both the defender and the advocate act as guidance for the judges, who will weigh them carefully, but may dismiss them as irrelevant.

In most tribunals, three judges will examine and pass judgment on each case. The majority verdict prevails. It is then the task of one of them to write the sentence; that is, to explain the rationale behind the decision which has been reached. If one judge does not agree with the other two, he may choose to write a dissenting judgment explaining why he disagrees. This dissenting judgment will be included with the other papers, but the majority verdict still holds.

In each case, the judges really need to make two decisions. Before they can judge on the validity of the marriage, they have to be morally certain that the truth of the matter is before them. Without that certainty, they cannot proceed to the judgment regarding validity.

The judges can only draw their opinions from the written evidence and written arguments before them. There is no sense in which anyone else may be present to argue either for or against the application.

Many tribunals will ask one judge, known as the instructing judge, to follow the case from the start. It will be his duty to ensure that the case is not unduly delayed at any stage of the process. He may well take responsibility for ensuring that the parties are kept informed of the progress of the case, and that they are briefed about the value of the evidence collected. He may take it upon himself to request that further evidence be collected before the case proceeds to the advocate.

It is worth pointing out again that it is the marriage and not either of the parties which is under investigation. Nevertheless, the nature of the matter means that one party may well feel that his or her rights are being jeopardised. Whilst the advocate's role can appear to be that of supporting the petitioner, the defender's role is one of supporting the sacrament of marriage. This may or may not coincide with the wishes of the respondent. Hence, the respondent may also appoint an advocate.

Sometimes the parties choose to be represented by a procurator, who stands in for them. The same person may serve as advocate and as procurator.

Chapter Twenty-One

Judgment and Appeal

The law presumes that the marriage is valid until such time as it is declared otherwise. Hence, the judges are asked to decide if the evidence before them is sufficient to reverse this presumption. Thus, typical examples of the questions which the judges must consider are:

- Is it proved that this marriage is invalid on the ground that the petitioner was gravely lacking in discretion of judgment regarding the essential rights and obligations of marriage?
- Is it proved that this marriage is invalid on the ground that the respondent had an intention against children?

The answer given by the judges must be either that invalidity is proved or that invalidity is not proved. Hence, in a case which does not succeed, the judges are not pronouncing that the marriage is valid, but that it is not proved that the marriage is invalid. The presumption of the law that the marriage is valid remains in force, but the possibility that that presumption is wrong is not denied.

> Xerxes met Zelda and instantly fell in love with her. She was stunningly beautiful and Xerxes could not believe it when Zelda seemed to reciprocate his feelings for her. Their relationship developed quickly.
>
> As they grew to know one another, Zelda told Xerxes that she had no relatives. She was an only child of parents who had themselves been only children. They had died two years earlier in a car accident. She had recently moved into the area and had very few friends.
>
> Xerxes proposed to Zelda within weeks and they decided to marry quickly. Six months after the wedding, Xerxes was searching for some documents and came across some belonging to Zelda which referred to a man called Callistus. He asked Zelda what they were about,

whereupon Zelda told him that Callistus and she were the same person. She had had a sex change operation two years before she met Xerxes. He was absolutely devastated by the news and decided that his only option was to leave her.

Five years later he met a Catholic girl and, desiring to marry her, petitioned for a declaration of invalidity of his marriage to Zelda, from whom he was already civilly divorced. The problem was that he could find no witnesses to support his allegation that Zelda was born a male. Zelda had herself taken the documents he had found and he did not now know where she was. When the case came to judgment, the judges had no more evidence than the somewhat bizarre story told by Xerxes. They could only conclude that nullity was not proved.

Two years later, quite by chance, Xerxes met Zelda again and she agreed to provide documentary evidence of her operation. When Xerxes again petitioned for nullity, the application was granted.

Xerxes's application failed initially because there was insufficient evidence for the judges to be sure that the story he told was true. Their pronouncement that the case was not proved did not amount to a declaration that the marriage was valid. Such a declaration would have been incorrect, as the subsequent granting of his application was to show. The initial declaration of the judges amounted to nothing more than a confirmation, for this particular marriage, of the presumption that all marriages are valid until declared otherwise.

If the decision of the judges is that the marriage is invalid, it is not the end of the matter. The case must then be sent to another tribunal for the decision to be confirmed. This amounts to an automatic appeal against the first decision. This second instance, whereby another tribunal is also to pass judgment, is another expression of the gravity of declaring a marriage invalid.

The judges of the appeal tribunal will examine the case quickly. They will take account of any additional comments made by the defender of the bond, or evidence collected after the first judgment. Initially, they have two choices: either confirm the decision of the first instance tribunal, or request that further work be carried out before they pronounce judgment. This further work can be anything from requesting a single document, to having the parties and all the witnesses re-interviewed. Their task is the same as that at first instance. They must be sure both that the truth of the matter is before them and that those facts amount to an invalid marriage.

If the appeal judges are satisfied that the first instance decision is right, then the appeal tribunal will issue a decree of confirmation of nullity. If, after all their deliberations, the appeal judges cannot agree with the first instance decision, the case must be sent to another tribunal for a third decision. This will usually be the Roman Rota, although a petition can be sent requesting that a more local tribunal be appointed as third instance tribunal for the particular case. This petition is by no means always granted.

If the decision of the first instance tribunal is that nullity is not proved, both of the parties have the right to appeal. If one of them chooses to exercise that right, the case will be sent to the appeal tribunal, which will examine it in much the same way as a successful application.

This system of appeals sounds more complicated than it is. Put simply, a successful application for nullity using the formal process (see Chapter 16) will have had at least one ground proved in two different tribunals. Using the documentary process, nullity is much more easily proved and not subject to the same possibility of human error. Consequently, a decree of nullity is granted without the need to appeal to another tribunal.

Generally speaking, a declaration of nullity leaves both parties free to enter a new marriage with the blessing of the Church, or to have an existing civil marriage recognised by the Church. However, in some situations, one or both parties may be prohibited from entering marriage. More is said about that in the next chapter.

In the event that nullity is not proved, the right to present a new petition can be exercised. However, unless there is new evidence which indicates that the first decision was wrong, the tribunal is likely to reject the petition at the beginning of the process.

The tribunal process will never solve all the problems which can arise from a broken marriage. Petitioners whose applications fail are advised to seek spiritual guidance and counselling to assist them in an understanding of their situation. More will be said about this in a later chapter.

Chapter Twenty-Two

Other Matters Arising From Nullity

Remarriage

When the nullity of a marriage is declared, the tribunal will not only pronounce judgment on the marriage but will also look to the future and the possibility of remarriage.

If the circumstances of the first marriage suggest that one or both parties might have difficulties in a second marriage, the judges will often make some recommendations concerning any possible future marriage. An obvious example might be when one of the parties suffers from a grave mental illness or a serious personality disorder. In other circumstances, the problem which led to the failure of the first union might only have been temporary and there would be no reason why a second successful union could not be formed. In such a case, the recommendation might be that one or both seek some sort of counselling before remarrying.

When it has been shown that one or both of the parties suffers from a psychological problem that has not been treated successfully, a prohibition against entering marriage will be laid down until such time as medical evidence is available to show that the problem has been overcome. Such prohibitions are not made unless the problem is likely to affect a future spouse and, thus, jeopardise the chance of a second union being successful. Of course, this is only a recommendation of the Church and if the party in question decided to marry outside the Church the prohibition would have no effect.

Time and Costs

If the tribunal system consistently fails in anything, it is in processing cases quickly and efficiently. Canon law suggests that tribunals should process a case in first instance within one year, and in each subsequent instance within a further six months. Some tribunals are able to act within these limits, but many seem unable to do so. Regrettably, some dioceses are taking three, four or even five years to process applications.

Some bishops have been unable to equip their tribunals with the personnel necessary to process applications quickly. Others simply do not have the personnel or resources available. As the proportion of marriages breaking down increases, so the number of applications for marriage nullity must increase. Bishops will inevitably find that they have an uphill task ensuring their tribunals have adequate resources.

Naturally, some cases can be processed more quickly than others. Most tribunals will have developed their own systems for controlling the flow of cases, which may number several hundred at one time. With so many, it is impossible to monitor each case all the time, and it is only with periodic checks that a case may come to light which has not progressed for some months.

The systems devised by tribunals will ensure that each case steadily progresses through the process. When a case is delayed for any reason, it is usually because the petitioner or respondent has been asked to furnish further information and no reply has been forthcoming. Failure to answer letters on time does seem to be a major cause of cases being delayed.

Unfortunately, processing applications for marriage nullity is expensive. Salaries have to be paid, and even the clergy and religious sisters and brothers have to have some source of income. There are also administrative and establishment expenses to be met: heating, lighting, secretarial costs, rent and rates, telephones, postage, stationery, office equipment and furniture. There is a considerable amount of work and expense involved in processing applications.

Most tribunals attempt to fund some of these expenses by asking petitioners for a contribution towards the cost of their applications. However, it is important to understand that declarations of nullity are not bought and sold. Any payments made are only a contribution towards the cost of undertaking the work. It has been known for people to object to the principle of having to pay. In fact, the cost of having the marriage declared null is small compared to the average cost of a wedding.

It is impossible to say what is the actual cost of processing an application for nullity, although it will almost certainly run into several hundred pounds, and possibly more. Each tribunal will have its own policy regarding its approach to petitioners for a contribution to the cost. Most tribunals are willing to accept that not everyone can afford to pay towards an application, and in a genuine case of hardship only a minimal contribution would be requested. It would seem safe to say that nobody should be deterred from making an application simply because of an inability to pay. Any petitioner who is worried about costs should approach the appropriate tribunal for further information.

Status of Children

A common question, asked by those whose marriages fail after the birth of children, is: "Won't a declaration of nullity make my children illegitimate? For surely if having the marriage declared null and void is saying we were never married, that means the children were born outside marriage?"

Much of the social stigma of being illegitimate has now evaporated and, certainly in the Church, the legal status of children is of no relevance to anything. Until recently, if a woman became pregnant outside marriage, the couple often rushed to marry before the child was born. It didn't seem to matter that the child was conceived outside marriage, as long as the birth occurred within marriage.

Legitimacy is concerned with the legal status of children. The term "legitimate" means within the law. Hence, in this context "illegitimate" means outside a lawful marriage. It does *not* mean outside a valid marriage. A marriage which is later declared invalid is nevertheless lawful until such time as the nullity is declared. Hence, even though invalid, it is still lawful and children born within that marriage are born within the law; that is, they are legitimate. The subsequent declaration that the marriage was null does not change the status of the children. Despite the fact that the marriage is declared to have been invalid from the start, it was still a legal marriage from the date of the wedding to the date of the nullity being granted.

It can be said with certainty that some marriages in which the couple rushed to marry because she was pregnant are invalid, although they have never been declared as such and so are legally presumed valid. The children of the marriage are legitimate, as is the marriage itself. If the marriage is later declared invalid, it only ceases to be a lawful marriage from the date of the decree of nullity.

It is worth stating again that even happy and successful marriages can be technically invalid. God is above the law, and if he chooses to bless a marriage, it could be irrelevant whether or not it is valid. It is only in attempting to solve problems arising from our humanity that the question of validity becomes important.

A Pastoral Note

The tribunal system and marriage nullity process often receive a bad press. The procedure is sometimes perceived as excessively secretive, extremely slow, a waste of human and other resources, and unpleasantly intrusive. Unfortunately, these criticisms are not always without foundation. Tribunal personnel will attempt to handle cases with sympathy and understanding, but they are not infallible.

The process of declaring a marriage invalid is a judicial process. The tribunal judges would be neglecting their duty and the trust placed in them by their bishop if they did not apply the law equitably and justly. In their approach to the parties, they will be pastoral and sensitive. However, when it comes to making a judicial decision, they are seeking truth. That means that some applications for nullity will not fulfil the requirements of the law for a decree of nullity to be granted.

The system is not so much secretive, as confidential. Petitioners, respondents and witnesses may prefer to make statements that they would not wish to become public knowledge, and in its search for truth the tribunal can allow confidential statements to be made, sometimes at the expense of the process appearing secretive. The reluctance of tribunal staff to risk giving petitioners false hope may also result in the appearance of secrecy.

There is no doubt that some people have had legitimate cause to complain about the way their applications have been handled by tribunals. However, there is also no doubt that many more have benefited greatly from being able to talk openly and honestly about their failed marriages, realising that they are not unique in the pain they endured in marriage and its breakdown, and being freed to search for God's will in a new relationship, if the application is successful.

128

The process is not without some discomfort or even pain, but the potential for healing is enormous.

Section III

Chapter Twenty-Three
Particular Situations

Non-consummation and Petrine Privilege Cases

There are certain broken marriages from which it is possible to remarry without the first having to be declared invalid. However, it is still necessary to have the first marriage examined by the Church before permission will be given to enter a second marriage. The Church will want to be sure that the circumstances of the broken marriage are appropriate to the particular conditions for these special cases to apply. The marriages, from which remarriage is possible without a declaration of nullity, are those that have never been consummated and marriages in which one or both of the parties was not baptised.

Since these cases do not involve a declaration of invalidity, it can be said that they are as near to divorce as it is possible to come in the Catholic Church. Christ taught that divorce is not possible. Yet he also gave Peter, the apostle, and his successors, the Popes, the power to bind and to loose (hence the name Petrine Privilege cases). It is only the Holy Father who is able to grant these privileges, which amount to a dissolution of the bond of the marriage using his power to bind and to loose. Thus, the first marriage is not declared invalid, although it may well be so. The bond of the first marriage is dissolved and the parties are declared free to enter a second union.

Cases involving non-consummation are not uncommon. However, few are actually processed using the special procedures laid down for such cases. Consummation of a marriage is considered essential to its fullness. Unless the two become one body, they are not married in the full sense of the word. When a non-consummated marriage breaks down, one or both of the parties can request that the Church dissolve the bond of that marriage by using the special procedures laid down for such cases.

Although it is the Holy Father who grants the dissolution, it is the local bishop or his delegate who is responsible for accumulating the evidence and preparing the case. The procedures are such that the fact of the non-consummation must be proved beyond reasonable doubt. It is beyond the scope of this book to give a detailed analysis of the evidence required, but suffice it to say there is no escaping the necessity for personal and intimate questions, and sometimes also the use of medical experts. These matters are by their nature intrusive, and so petitioners usually prefer to petition for a decree of nullity, rather than for a dissolution. Nevertheless, the petitioner would have the right to present a petition for a dissolution, if preferred.

Note, if the case is considered as an application for nullity, it is not the fact of non-consummation which would make the marriage invalid, but the cause of the failure to consummate the marriage. Personal questions would still have to be asked, but not to the same extent as required for a dissolution.

When an application for nullity is presented for a marriage in which one of the parties was not baptised, a dissolution is also possible in certain circumstances. According to the Church's teaching, only a sacramental marriage may not be dissolved. Thus, if one of the parties is not baptised, the marriage is not considered sacramental. A sacrament is, after all, exclusively a sign. The reality which it signifies does not depend on that sign. If a person is not baptised, it is assumed that he or she is not a Christian and so would not signal Christian beliefs. Where baptisms have become less of a social necessity in some countries, the incidence of such cases is bound to rise.

Again, these marriages are dissolved only by the Holy Father. The case is prepared locally, and the papers are then forwarded to Rome. Such applications are not always granted.

The important distinction to bear in mind is that these are dissolutions and not declarations of invalidity. The Church presumes that a valid bond of marriage exists and the Holy Father uses his office to dissolve that bond. Thus, what is requested by the petitioner is a favour of the Holy Father.

Procedures have been laid down as to the correct way to present an application for a dissolution of the bond of a non-sacramental marriage. These procedures also give guidance as to the factors which will be taken into account for the favour to be granted. For example, it is desirable that no scandal be caused by the granting of the favour, that there be some reason for considering the marriage in any case to be invalid, and that the petitioner was not the cause of the marriage breaking down (even though this could give rise to the anomalous situation that the granting of the favour might depend on which of the couple made the application, rather than the merit of the case). It is also desired that it be for the personal good of the Catholic that the dissolution be granted.

Pauline Privilege Cases

There is another method of dissolving the bond of a non-sacramental marriage when that marriage is between two people who are not baptised. The principle is found in St Paul's First Letter to the Corinthians (7:12–16), and hence is known as the Pauline Privilege. This allows one of the parties to become baptised and enter a second marriage providing he or she does not continue with the first marriage after the baptism, and providing the other party does not wish to continue with the marriage. It is usually assumed that the adoption of the Christian faith is a source of dispute in the first marriage, and may even be the reason for its failure. However, this is not an essential condition for the use of this privilege.

It is best illustrated by an example:

> Octavius and Nocturna, neither baptised, were married for four years before they separated. Octavius had met another woman and continued his infidelity despite Nocturna threatening to leave. So she did.

> Two years later, Nocturna began to take an interest in Christianity, and was later received into the Church. She met Paulinus, a Catholic man, and they fell in love and wished to marry. The local bishop, having determined that all the conditions for the Pauline Privilege were fulfilled, gave permission for the marriage to proceed. The bond of Nocturna's marriage to Octavius was dissolved by the event of her marriage to Paulinus.

Note, in this case, that the dissolution is brought about by the second marriage taking place, and not from the use of the Petrine privilege or any other special power of the Church. It is only required that the Church ensure that the conditions for use of the privilege are fulfilled. The implicit assumption here is that the faith of a believer is more important than the bond of the first non-sacramental marriage.

Multiple Marriages

When there have been two or more previous civil marriages, the situation can become complicated. Thankfully, for a Catholic, the question of multiple marriages should not arise. Any Catholic wishing to remarry should first have obtained a decree of nullity of the first marriage. Theoretically, there is no limit to the number of declarations of nullity of marriage which a person can obtain. However, in practice, a person who is approaching the Church for a second or third time would be asked to consider the possibility that entering yet another marriage is more likely to create a situation for harm than one for the well-being of the persons concerned.

The problem of multiple marriages really only arises when a Catholic wishes to marry a non-Catholic who has been married more than once before. There are two schools of thought about how these situations should be handled. Both have sound arguments to support them, but only one is always practicable.

The legal approach starts from the premise that all marriages are valid until declared otherwise. Hence, the problem of multiple marriages does not arise. The first marriage is considered valid unless a declaration of nullity is granted. Hence, any subsequent marriage is automatically invalid because of the impediment arising from the bond of the first marriage.

Take the example of Heather, a non-Catholic, who married and divorced in turn Isaac, Jacob, and Kenneth, all of whom were non-Catholics. She then wished to marry Lawrence, a Catholic. The Church can begin by declaring invalid her marriages to Jacob and Kenneth because she was bound by the marriage promises she made to Isaac. It is only the validity of her marriage to Isaac which needs to be examined. If that is found to be invalid, she would be free to marry Lawrence in the Church.

The more theological approach, applied where possible, looks at the reality which lies behind all the legal presumptions (e.g. that a marriage is presumed valid) and argues that, if there is an invalid marriage, then there is no bond preventing entry to another marriage.

In other words, the bond of marriage only arises if there is a valid marriage. If the first marriage is invalid, the second marriage may be valid by default.

Thus, if Heather's marriage to Isaac is invalid, then there was no impediment to her marrying Jacob, and her promises to Jacob could be presumed valid. If that presumption was found to be false (by a separate investigation into the second union), and her marriage to Jacob was also invalid, there was no reason why she was not free to marry Kenneth. Hence, it is argued, the correct way to approach her proposed marriage to Lawrence is to examine in turn each of her former marriages. Only in the event that each was invalid would she be free to marry Lawrence.

In the example given, this approach, although somewhat long-winded, is nevertheless possible. However, in some cases it is not possible to examine previous marriages.

Consider, for example, the possibility that Isaac had been married before he married Heather. In theory, using this second approach to multiple marriages, the Church would have to examine Isaac's first marriage before examining the marriage between Heather and Isaac. However, unless Isaac or his first wife was willing to co-operate in that investigation, it would be impossible to examine their marriage for possible invalidity. The legal approach to this situation would be to say that Heather was not bound by her marriage promises to Isaac, because he was already bound by promises to his first wife. Consequently, Heather is free to marry Lawrence in the Church providing she can have her marriage to Isaac declared invalid, which should be a simple matter.

However, the Church is actually likely to use a combination of the legal and the theological approaches. A documentary process will be used to declare invalid her marriage to Isaac, but her marriages to Jacob and Kenneth would both be subject to a formal judicial process to determine if they were invalid. Only if these processes were successful would Heather be declared free to marry Lawrence.

The Impossible Situation

Throughout everything that has been said so far, it has always been assumed that either a nullity or a dissolution was possible. Mention has been made of the fact that applications for nullity can fail, but nothing has been said of the consequences of such failure.

The process of declaring a marriage invalid is judicial by nature. In order for that judgement to be made, there has to be a degree of certainty that the marriage is invalid. It can, however, happen that, although a marriage is invalid, the evidence of invalidity is simply not available. It is also possible that a marriage which is capable of being declared invalid is not put to the test, perhaps because neither party feels that a declaration of nullity would prove beneficial, or because the parties feel psychologically unable to bring themselves to petition for it. It is also possible that the first marriage is simply not invalid, although the Church has no mechanism for stating this. Church law already presumes that the marriage is not invalid.

Some people are quite content to live a single life after marriage breakdown. Others are not. In the latter case, when the law is unable to provide a practical solution to a desire to remarry or to have a second marriage recognised, the Church has to attempt to find some sort of pastoral solution, which recognises both the spirit of the gospel and the conscience of the individual.

The final chapter considers these "impossible situations" in more detail. These are situations in which a couple find themselves in an irregular union; that is, one which the Church does not officially recognise, usually because one or both parties have been previously married and the former spouse is still alive. The Church does not offer specific official norms on these matters, apart from encouraging such couples to play as full a part in the Church as their circumstances allow. It represents something of a grey area, in part because of a fear of appearing to water down Christ's teaching that marriage is permanent. The content of the next chapter is not, then, official Church teaching, but an overview of the pastoral approaches adopted by certain bishops to those in irregular unions. The Church would always see its primary concern as to encourage couples to enter only a permanent, God-made union.

Chapter Twenty-Four

Irregular Unions

Priests and others who regularly offer spiritual guidance to individuals will sometimes find themselves with the apparent dilemma of trying to reconcile pastoral practice with official Church teaching. How do you respond to a woman who says that she regularly uses contraception, and feels that God understands? What do you say to the man who is asking to receive the sacraments, when he is in his second marriage?

The fundamental problem in these cases is the reconciliation of the internal and external fora. From the point of view of the individual, he or she feels that God at least does not disapprove of something which appears to be against the teaching of the Church. From the point of view of the minister, if the person's conscience is not telling him or her that it is wrong, should the minister disturb that conscience? After all, one way in which God speaks to us is through our consciences (Vatican II, *Gaudium et spes*, n.16). The minister who intervenes in such matters could risk making himself a judge over God.

Matters of individual conscience are sometimes referred to as matters of the internal forum. Canon law and Church teaching in general apply first of all to the external forum, but nevertheless they seek to influence and inform the internal forum.

Solutions at the level of the internal forum can be applied to a number of pastoral problems. However, the so-called *internal forum solution* is a phrase which has become widely used for one particular approach to those who are in irregular unions, such as second marriages, and who would not normally expect to be able to receive the sacraments. When such difficulties arise, the Church will first attempt to find a solution which is acceptable in both the internal and the external fora.

The obvious solution is to obtain a declaration of nullity, if such is possible. Other solutions which form part of the Church's recommended practice (see for example, Pope John Paul II's Apostolic Exhortation, *Familiaris consortio*, n.84) are for the couple to recognise the irregularity of their union and to distance themselves from any contradiction with the full practice of their faith. For some couples, this could mean living apart or, if that is not possible, living without that physical relationship which is proper to married couples (the so-called solution of "living as brother and sister").

However, it is not always possible for a couple in an irregular union to adopt a solution such as living apart, living without that physical relationship proper to marriage, or obtaining a declaration of nullity and having their marriage recognised by the Church. Nor is it helpful to stand in judgment over these couples, saying they knew what they were doing when they entered the irregular union and now they must suffer the consequences.

Many couples in this situation did not fully understand the consequences of their actions, or perhaps even entered marriage believing mistakenly that it was a union recognised by the Church. Examples of people who might unwittingly find themselves in this position are those who convert to Catholicism whilst in a marriage which the Catholic Church does not recognise, or Catholics who have entered an irregular union at a time of spiritual poverty.

The *internal forum solution* might be of some assistance to those unable to find a solution in the external forum. However, in its strict interpretation, it is not available to everyone in a second union. Nor is it a way to avoid or put aside Church teaching. It is a recognition of the limitations of the various external forum solutions. Since it is a matter of the internal forum, it is first and foremost a matter between God and the couple. The Church's involvement consists in helping the couple to make *their* decision.

Recourse to an *internal forum solution* does not mean that a previously irregular union becomes a marriage recognised by the Church. However, it does effectively amount to a statement that, although the Church cannot give official recognition to the irregular marriage, it is at least open to the possibility that the parties living in that union are not living a life which is contrary to the gospel.

Hence, an *internal forum solution* will never include a ceremony of blessing or exchange of consent, or anything which gives the appearance of officially recognising the marriage. Consequently, it is not a perfect solution. It does not resolve the problem of the marriage being irregular, but of the inability to receive the sacrament of the Eucharist, which is something that would normally arise from an irregular union.

It is a pastoral solution, and the decision to use it should only be made by those who are competent. Thus, it is usually only applied after a period of consultation between the couple and their priest. He will seek to ensure that the couple are properly disposed, that they understand what the *solution* is and how it will be applied in their particular circumstances, and that they have exhausted any possible solutions of the external forum. Without such care being taken, there is a danger that the *solution* will be seen as dispensing with Christ's teaching that marriage is for life.

The following conditions would be considered necessary for any possible application of the *internal forum solution*:

- The couple and the priest must be convinced of the invalidity of the first marriage, even though a formal declaration of nullity is not possible. [Obviously, since the *internal forum solution* applies when an external forum solution, such as nullity, is not possible, the proof required here is less than that required for a formal declaration of nullity. The minister could rely on the good faith of the couple.]
- The parties must be able to receive the sacraments without causing scandal or adverse criticism amongst the faithful.
- The parties must promise to validate the marriage in the event of the death of the former spouse(s).
- The parties must fulfil the responsibilities of Christian marriage in the present union; that is, practise fidelity, parental responsibility and seek to build an appropriate community of life and love.
- The Catholic party must have continued to practise the Catholic faith as far as possible and, if appropriate, any children of the union should be raised in the Catholic faith.
- The sacraments must be received in a church where the irregularity of the union is unknown, if this is the only way of avoiding scandal.

- The couple must be willing to live without Church approval of their union, even though this does not imply disapproval of their reception of the sacraments.

This is the strict interpretation of the *internal forum solution*. Clearly it has its limitations. For example, most couples would not be in a position to judge the validity of a marriage, and priests who have not had specialist training are also prone to error when it comes to making such judgments.

It is also difficult to determine when scandal is being given. The danger of scandal arises when a pastoral decision can be misinterpreted as condoning an action which appears contrary to the gospel or church teaching. However, there is also a danger that the possibility of scandal is used as an excuse not to apply basic gospel values of love, mercy and forgiveness, when such application might be misunderstood. Such failure can itself be a cause for scandal. The priest can find himself in the position of appearing to condemn a person who has done nothing more than follow his or her conscience. There might also be more scandal involved in a couple feeling rejected by their parish community than there would be in allowing them to receive the sacraments in their own parish. Consequently, those involved in applying the *internal forum solution* will need to tread warily.

One difficulty in applying the strict conditions for the use of the *internal forum solution* is that it is not always practicable for these judgments to be made using purely canonical principles. In some cases, the principles to be used might be pastoral in nature, such as the following:

- Were all reasonable steps taken to ensure the success of the first marriage? [This is a guide to the respect of the parties for the principles of Christian marriage. It is not an excuse, for example, to refuse the *internal forum solution* in a case when one of the parties was responsible for the first marriage failing.]
- Are the couple living in good conscience regarding the second union; in other words, do they feel at peace with God in their second union?
- Have the couple shown a desire for commitment by at least entering a civil marriage?

- Are they showing stability in this civil marriage and, but for the irregularity of their union, in all other ways giving good Christian example? In other words, does the marriage show external signs of sacramentality; are the couple apparently acting under the prompting of the Holy Spirit; does this union give the appearance of having been blessed by God?
- Are they fulfilling any natural obligations towards others arising from any previous union?

This, however, still leaves a problem. The *internal forum solution*, in its strict interpretation, is not going to help everyone who is in an irregular union and to whom an external forum solution is not available. The Church cannot have a ready answer for all these people. The assumption is that they are breaking the law of Christ, as well as the sixth commandment, and so cannot be admitted to the sacraments.

St Paul tells us "... neither death nor life, no angel, no prince, nothing that exists, nothing still to come, not any power, or height or depth, nor any created thing, can ever come between us and the love of God made visible in Jesus Christ" (*Romans* 8:38–39). If, then, nothing can come between us and the love of God, can it be possible for a Christian to find himself or herself in a state of permanent banishment from the sacraments?

Certainly, canon law envisages offences which are considered so serious that a person committing them is subject to excommunication, either automatically or after a formal judicial enquiry. Formally declared excommunication is more than a temporary need to seek absolution before receiving the Eucharist after committing a grave sin. A formally excommunicated person is not even allowed public association with the Church until such time as the censure is lifted. However, provided certain conditions are fulfilled, there is no reason why full communion cannot be restored.

The offences which justify formal excommunication are far more serious than those which are being considered here, and great care must be taken that there is no confusion between those who are excommunicated, and those who are welcome as part of the Church community but do not receive the Eucharist. Excommunication might be imposed upon those who commit heresy, who knowingly desecrate the Eucharist, or who, for purely selfish motives, freely assist in an abortion (but even then there are frequently circumstances which mitigate against the application of formal excommunication). These actions are offences against humanity, or can cause grave harm to the faithful. When two people are living in a loving and life-giving relationship, the offence of their union being irregular is hardly comparable, assuming there was no great scandal in their coming together.

The Holy See has issued guidance to the bishops of the Catholic Church concerning the reception of the Eucharist by those who are divorced and who have remarried without Church approval; in other words, those in irregular unions. Obviously the norms do not apply to those who are simply separated or divorced, and who have not entered a second union. The general guideline for those in irregular unions is that reception of the Eucharist is not possible.

This guidance, which applies only to situations in which the first union was a valid marriage, could give the impression of denying the use of the *internal forum solution* as an appropriate means of helping some of those who are in an irregular union. Such an interpretation is inappropriate, however, as will be explained in the following paragraphs.

The guidance is restrictive in that it denies the exercise of the right to the sacraments to certain members of the faithful; a right which is acknowledged in the documents of Vatican II (*Lumen Gentium*, n.37). Canon law lays down a principle to be followed in interpreting laws which restrict the free exercise of rights. They are to be interpreted strictly [canon 18]. The guidance issued by the Holy See is not law as such. Nevertheless, because it restricts the exercise of rights, it too is to be interpreted strictly; that is, it will apply only when all the conditions laid down in the guidance are fulfilled. One of the conditions for exclusion from the Eucharist is that the first marriage was valid.

The guidance is based on the assumption that all marriages are valid. If such valid marriages are God-made unions then they are permanent, and consequently remarriage is never possible as long as the bond of the first marriage remains. However, the Church has no mechanism, other than the informed conscience of an individual, for knowing God's uniting force in that person's marriage. The fact that a couple exchanged vows in a wedding ceremony does not necessarily mean that God has united them. Consequently, if someone can enter a second union in good conscience, which is a condition for the use of the *internal forum solution*, that person would be effectively expressing the belief that the first marriage was not a God-made union.

Based on Christ's teaching regarding the permanence of marriage, the Church would argue that couples in irregular unions are, by definition, living in a state and condition of life which is not compatible with the Church as a whole. The Eucharist is the sacrament of the unity of the Church and cannot be separated from the sacrament of union with Christ, who is the Head of the Church. For this reason, reception of the Eucharist is inappropriate for those living in irregular unions. However, where a priest or bishop judges that the use of the *internal forum solution* would be appropriate for a particular couple, he is making a judgment that, despite the technical irregularity of their union, that couple are not in fact living in a state and condition of life which sets them apart from the rest of the Church. This could be an application of the principle of subsidiarity. In this case, the Church, being the local Church, does not consider a particular couple to be separated from the Body of Christ, despite the irregularity of their union. In such circumstances, reception of the Eucharist would not always be inappropriate.

In all of these matters, the Church is concerned that the faithful should not be led into error and confusion regarding the Church's teaching and the indissolubility of marriage. At the same time, the recognition by many bishops and priests of the need for and use of the *internal forum solution*, and the more general need to give sound pastoral guidance and bring Christ's peace and reconciliation to those wounded by marriage breakdown, has led to an urgent need to teach the faithful specifically about marriage and the effects of marriage breakdown, but more generally about basic gospel values of love, mercy and forgiveness, and the need to avoid judging others.

The use of the *internal forum solution* conforms with canon law regarding those who may receive the Eucharist. Members of the Church have a right to the sacraments [canon 213] and, specifically, "any baptised person who is not forbidden by law may and must be admitted to Holy Communion" [canon 912]. Amongst those forbidden by law are those who "obstinately persist in a manifest grave sin" [canon 915]. Again, as a restrictive canon, this is to be interpreted strictly. A manifest sin is a sin which is publicly known. Obstinate persistence would occur when a person continues with the sin, refusing to heed warnings from the appropriate ecclesiastical authorities or Church teaching. The canon can apply only when all those conditions are met. Any doubt should prevent the use of the canon. The presence of a grave sin has to be established. It has to be manifest, and there has to be obstinate persistence with it. If there is doubt about the application of any of these, the restriction cannot be assumed to apply. If the conditions for use of the *internal forum solution* are adhered to, there will always remain some doubt that the conditions for the application of this canon have been met. In such circumstances, reception of the Eucharist should not be forbidden.

Finally, the *internal forum solution* for those in irregular unions was acknowledged by the Congregation for the Doctrine of the Faith in a letter in April 1973 to all local Ordinaries. In it, the Congregation stressed the Church's teaching regarding the indissolubility of marriage and the discipline regarding admission to the sacraments of those living in an irregular union. On this latter point, the letter stated: "With regard to admission to the sacraments, the local Ordinaries will also please, on the one hand, stress observance of the current discipline of the Church while, on the other hand, take care that pastors of souls follow up with particular solicitude those who are living in an irregular union and, in such cases, in addition to other correct means, use the approved practice of the Church in the internal forum" [unofficial translation]. This teaching has been refined in subsequent documents, the latest of which was issued in September 1994.

But there are those for whom an *internal forum solution* is not the answer. Many Catholics freely choose to enter a second marriage when the first one breaks down. For some, it is a moment of crisis of faith. They feel they have to make a choice between their faith and second marriage. For some people, when faith seems to stand in the way of personal happiness, it can be difficult to accept that faith is right.

For some of these people, the choice of a second marriage amounts in their own eyes to a departure from the Church. Some do apply for nullity but, in spite of this, for one reason or another, a decree of nullity cannot be granted. Others simply do not try, feeling that they do not need the approval of the Church to take such a step. If they are living in this second union in good conscience, does the Church have the right to suggest that they are living in a state of sin? Surely, in an individual case, that is a judgment that only God or the individual can make, even if some appropriate pastoral intervention might be necessary if scandal is being given.

The following is a fairly typical example of a situation in which it might not be possible to obtain a decree of nullity:

> Delilah and Eric had been married for fourteen years when Eric left to go and live with his secretary. Delilah knew their marriage was not wonderful, but she did not think it was that bad either. It had started off well enough, and only in the last five years did they seem not to have time for one another. His job had been so demanding.

> She would have preferred that he had talked of his unhappiness rather than just go off, but they had never really been able to share their deepest feelings and emotions. She went to her priest for some help, but found him unsympathetic. She stopped going to church.

> After a few years she found herself attracted to another man. He had never been married and was showing a lot of interest in her. Eventually, she decided to marry him. Two years later, and happy in her second marriage, she decided that she wanted to return to the practice of her faith.

Delilah's experience is not uncommon. Assuming there were no other facts which are relevant, any petition for a decree of nullity would probably fail. For the same reason, the *internal forum solution* would probably not apply, because there is no obvious reason why the first marriage might be invalid. Delilah seemingly finds herself in the position of having made a commitment to a man which will prevent her from receiving the sacraments.

The Church, on an official level, has no ready answer for her which will allow her both to receive the sacraments and respect the promises she has made to her second partner. It is possible to speculate as to how the Church might adopt new practices, such as those used by the Orthodox Churches, to assist some people, who find themselves in a situation similar to Delilah's, to return to the full practice of their faith. However, such speculation would not be helpful here.

The current practice of the Roman Catholic Church is for those who are in irregular unions, and who cannot obtain a declaration of nullity, to seek advice and guidance from an informed priest who might be able to help them in their quest to resolve any conflict between their faith and their situation in life. Suffice it to say, there are no easy and quick solutions to these conflicts. Recourse to the words of St Paul, already quoted in this chapter, might offer some comfort: "Nothing can ever come between us and the love of God" (*Romans* 8:39).

Appendix One
Tribunal Addresses

The addresses given below were correct at the time of going to press. In the event of failure to make contact using the address below, petitioners can write to their local bishop. Alternatively, parish priests should be able to assist with the address of the tribunal.

DIOCESES OF ENGLAND AND WALES

Arundel & Brighton	The Officialis Arundel and Brighton Tribunal Upper Drive Hove East Sussex BN3 6NE
Birmingham	The Officialis Birmingham Metropolitan Tribunal Archbishop's House St Chad's Queensway Birmingham B4 6EX
Brentwood	The Officialis Brentwood Marriage Tribunal Cathedral House Ingrave Road Brentwood Essex CM15 8AT
Cardiff	The Officialis Cardiff Marriage Tribunal The Presbytery Grand Avenue Ely Cardiff CF5 4HX

Clifton	The Officialis Clifton Marriage Tribunal Diocesan Offices Egerton Road Bishopston Bristol BS7 8HW
East Anglia	The Officialis East Anglia Tribunal The White House 21 Upgate Poringland Norwich NR14 7SH
Hallam	The Officialis Hallam Matrimonial Tribunal Hallam Pastoral Centre St Charles' Street Attercliffe Sheffield S9 2WU
Hexham and Newcastle	The Officialis Hexham and Newcastle Tribunal St Vincent's The Roman Way West Denton Newcastle-upon-Tyne NE15 7LT
Lancaster	The Officialis Lancaster Marriage Tribunal SS Mary and James Snow Hill Scorton Preston PR3 1AY
Leeds	The Officialis Leeds Diocesan Tribunal 7 St Mark's Avenue Leeds LS2 9BN

Liverpool	The Officialis Liverpool Metropolitan Tribunal 152 Brownlow Hill Liverpool L3 5RQ
Menevia	The Officialis Menevia Marriage Tribunal The Presbytery Our Lady of the Assumption Neath Road Briton Ferry West Glamorgan SA11 2YR
Middlesbrough	The Officialis Middlesbrough Diocesan Tribunal 50A The Avenue Linthorpe Middlesbrough Cleveland TS5 6QT
Northampton	The Officialis Northampton Marriage Tribunal Bishop's House Marriott Street Northampton NN2 6AW
Nottingham	The Officialis Nottingham Diocesan Tribunal Willson Square Derby Road Nottingham NG1 5AW
Plymouth	The Officialis Plymouth Diocesan Tribunal Rosary House Fore Street Heavitree Exeter EX1 2QH

Portsmouth	The Officialis Portsmouth Diocesan Tribunal St Mary's Road East Hendred Oxon OX12 8LF
Salford	The Officialis Salford Marriage Tribunal Curial Offices Cathedral House 250 Chapel Street Salford M3 5LL
Shrewsbury	The Officialis Shrewsbury Diocesan Tribunal Curial Offices 2 Park Road South Birkenhead L43 4UX
Southwark	The Officialis Southwark Marriage Tribunal 208 Sydenham Road London SE26 5SE
Westminster	The Officialis Westminster Metropolitan Tribunal Vaughan House 46 Francis Street London SWIP 1QN
Wrexham	The Officialis Wrexham Marriage Tribunal Bishop's House Sontley Road Wrexham Clwyd LL13 7EW

ALL SCOTTISH DIOCESES

The Officialis
Scottish National Tribunal
22 Woodrow Road
Glasgow G41 5PN

REGIONS OF IRELAND

Armagh

The Officialis
Armagh Marriage Tribunal
15 College Street
Armagh BT61 9BT

Cork

The Officialis
Regional Tribunal Offices
The Lough
Cork

Dublin

The Officialis
Dublin Regional Tribunal
The Diocesan Offices
Archbishop's House
Dublin 9

Galway

The Officialis
Galway Tribunal
7 Waterside
Woodquay
Galway

Appendix Two

Drafting a Petition

The following is an aid to writing a petition for an investigation into the validity of a marriage, should you wish to write your own. However, a formal petition drafted by yourself is not essential for an application. It would be sufficient for you to contact the tribunal and tell them you wish to apply for the nullity of your marriage.

The petition should be sent to a tribunal competent to hear the case (see page 102). For examples of a complete petition see pages 153 and 105. An example of an outline petition is given on the next page.

———————

Example of outline Petition

[*your full address,*
including postcode]

Dear Bishop/Archbishop/Cardinal [*give surname of bishop.*
Alternatively, use the more formal "My Lord" if a bishop; "Your
Grace" if an Archbishop; or "Your Eminence" if a Cardinal]

PETITION FOR MARRIAGE NULLITY

I, [*your current full name. If a woman state also your maiden name*],
married [*the full name of your former spouse*] on [*date of marriage*] at
[*give place of marriage. State also the denomination of any church*
e.g. All Saints Anglican Church]. At the time, I was [*age*] years old,
and s/he was [*age*] years old. I am a [*give denomination, e.g.*
Catholic], s/he is a [*denomination*]. We separated on [*date*] and were
divorced on [*date, or state if not yet divorced*].

In a few lines give some details about when you met, the courtship and
the decision to marry. Give some idea of the time scale involved, and
any other relevant and important details concerning your decision to
marry.

Give a few details about the marriage and the principal problems.
Give the names and dates of birth of any children. Give the reasons
which led to the separation.

Very brief details of any subsequent marriages should be given. Give
the reason for requesting a nullity.

End your petition like this:
"I, therefore, petition for an investigation into my marriage to [*name*
of former spouse] for possible invalidity in canon law."

Signature:............................... *Date:*...........................

153

Example of complete Petition

18 Higher London Boulevard
Edinburgh
EH45 7ZZ

Dear Bishop Smith,

PETITION FOR MARRIAGE NULLITY

I, Michael Maurice Minorca, married Jayne Jezebel Minorca (born Jupiter), on 12th July 1932 at the Catholic church of St Luke, Liverpool. At that time, I was twenty-four and she was twenty-three years old. We are both Catholics. We separated in July 1978, and were divorced on 23rd March 1981.

We met about three years before the marriage. We were working at the same place. Neither of us had much money and we tended to go for walks rather than go out socialising. We got engaged after a year, but didn't marry for another two years because we didn't have the money.

Our marriage was never wonderfully happy. We had two children before the war; born in August 1936 and February 1939. I was called up in early 1940 and was away for most of the next few years. We were both unfaithful in that time. However, after the war we seemed to settle down again. We always struggled for money until March 1978, when Jayne won £250,000 on the pools. She changed totally. She decided she was going to see the world and she wasn't taking me with her. She left in July 1978 and I haven't seen her since.

I have now met another lady and we want to get married. I, therefore, petition for an investigation into my marriage to Jayne Minorca for possible invalidity in canon law.

Yours sincerely,

M. M. Minorca
23rd November 1992

Some Canons to Which the Text Refers

The following canons are taken from *The Code of Canon Law in English Translation,* published in 1983. Only those canons, or extracts thereof, which are directly relevant to the chapters indicated, are reproduced.

CHAPTER 4

Canon 1060 – Marriage enjoys the favour of the law. Consequently, in doubt the validity of a marriage must be upheld until the contrary is proven.

Canon 1108,1 (extract) – Only those marriages are valid which are contracted in the presence of the local Ordinary or parish priest or of the priest or deacon delegated by either of them, who, in the presence of two witnesses, assists. . .

Canon 1108,2 – Only that person who, being present, asks the contracting parties to manifest their consent and in the name of the Church receives it, is understood to assist at a marriage.

Canon 1116,1 – If one who, in accordance with the law, is competent to assist, cannot be present or be approached without grave inconvenience, those who intend to enter a true marriage can validly and lawfully contract in the present of witnesses only: 1) in danger of death; 2) apart from danger of death, provided it is prudently foreseen that this state of affairs will continue for a month.

Canon 1116,2 – In either case, if another priest or deacon is at hand who can be present, he must be called upon and, together with the witnesses, be present at the celebration of the marriage, without prejudice to the validity of the marriage in the presence of only the witnesses.

CHAPTER 5

Canon 1057,1 – A marriage is brought into being by the lawfully manifested consent of persons who are legally capable. This consent cannot be supplied by any human power.

Canon 1057,2 – Matrimonial consent is an act of will by which a man and a woman by an irrevocable covenant mutually give and accept one another for the purpose of establishing a marriage.

CHAPTER 6

Canon 1059 – The marriage of Catholics, even if only one party is a Catholic, is governed not only by divine law but also by canon law, without prejudice to the competence of the civil authority in respect of the merely civil effects of the marriage.

Canon 1108 – see Chapter 4 above.

CHAPTER 7

Canon 1083,1 – A man cannot validly enter marriage before the completion of his sixteenth year of age, nor a woman before the completion of her fourteenth year.

Canon 1083,2 – The Episcopal Conference may establish a higher age for the lawful celebration of marriage.

Canon 1084,1 – Antecedent and perpetual impotence to have sexual intercourse, whether on the part of the man or on that of the woman, whether absolute or relative, by its very nature invalidates marriage.

Canon 1084,2 – If the impediment of impotence is doubtful, whether the doubt be one of law or one of fact, the marriage is not to be prevented nor, while the doubt persists, is it to be declared null.

Canon 1084,3 (extract) – ... sterility neither forbids nor invalidates a marriage.

Canon 1085,1 – A person bound by the bond of a previous marriage, even if not consummated, invalidly attempts marriage.

Canon 1085,2 – Even though the previous marriage is invalid or for any reason dissolved, it is not thereby lawful to contract another marriage before the nullity or the dissolution of the previous one has been established lawfully and with certainty.

Canon 1086,1 – A marriage is invalid when one of the two persons was baptised in the Catholic Church or received into it and has not by a formal act defected from it, and the other was not baptised.

[Canon 1086,2 mentions the conditions under which this impediment is dispensed. Canon 1086,3 refers to situations of doubt of the baptism of one of the parties.]

Canon 1087 – Those who are in sacred orders invalidly attempt marriage.

Canon 1088 – Those who are bound by a public perpetual vow of chastity in a religious institute invalidly attempt marriage.

Canon 1089 – No marriage can exist between a man and a woman who has been abducted, or at least detained, with a view to contracting a marriage with her, unless the woman, after she has been separated from her abductor and established in a safe and free place, chooses marriage of her own accord.

Canon 1090,1 – One who, with a view to entering marriage with a particular person, has killed that person's spouse, or his or her own spouse, invalidly attempts this marriage.

Canon 1090,2 – They also invalidly attempt marriage with each other who, by mutual physical or moral action, brought about the death of either's spouse.

Canon 1091,1 – Marriage is invalid between those related by consanguinity in all degrees of the direct line, whether ascending or descending, legitimate or natural.

Canon 1091,2 – In the collateral line, it is invalid up to the fourth degree inclusive.

Canon 1091,3 – The impediment of consanguinity is not multiplied.

Canon 1091,4 – A marriage is never to be permitted if a doubt exists as to whether the parties are related by consanguinity in any degree of the direct line, or in the second degree of the collateral line.

Canon 1092 – Affinity in any degree of the direct line invalidates marriage.

Canon 1093 – The impediment of public propriety arises when a couple live together after an invalid marriage, or from a notorious or public concubinage. It invalidates marriage in the first degree of the direct line between the man and those related by consanguinity to the woman, and vice versa.

Canon 1094 – Those who are legally related by reason of adoption cannot validly marry each other if their relationship is in the direct line or in the second degree of the collateral line.

CHAPTER 8

Canon 1096,1 – For matrimonial consent to exist, it is necessary that the contracting parties be at least not ignorant of the fact that marriage is a permanent partnership between a man and a woman, ordered to the procreation of children through some form of sexual co-operation.

Canon 1096,2 – This ignorance is not presumed after puberty.

Canon 1095 (extract) – The following are incapable of contracting marriage: those who lack sufficient use of reason.

CHAPTERS 9, 10 & 11

Canon 1095 (extract) – The following are incapable of contracting marriage: those who suffer from a grave lack of discretion of judgment concerning the essential matrimonial rights and obligations to be mutually given and accepted.

CHAPTER 12

Canon 1095 (extract) – The following are incapable of contracting marriage: those who, because of causes of a psychological nature, are unable to assume the essential obligations of marriage.

CHAPTER 13

Canon **1097,1** – Error of person renders a marriage invalid.

Canon **1097,2** – Error about a quality of the person, even though it be the reason for the contract, does not render a marriage invalid unless this quality is directly and principally intended.

Canon **1098** – A person contracts invalidly who enters marriage inveigled by deceit, perpetrated in order to secure consent, concerning some quality of the other party, which of its very nature can seriously disrupt the partnership of conjugal life.

CHAPTER 14

Canon **1101,1** – The internal consent of the mind is presumed to conform to the words or signs used in the celebration of a marriage.

Canon **1101,2** – If, however, either or both of the parties should by a positive act of the will exclude marriage itself or any essential element of marriage or any essential property, such party contracts invalidly.

CHAPTER 15

Canon **1102,1** – Marriage cannot be validly contracted subject to a condition concerning the future.

Canon **1102,2** – Marriage entered into subject to a condition concerning the past or the present is valid or not, according as whatever is the basis of the condition exists or not.

Canon **1102,3** – However, a condition as mentioned in 1102,2 may not lawfully be attached except with the written permission of the local Ordinary.

Canon **1103** – A marriage is invalid which was entered into by reason of force or of grave fear imposed from outside, even if not purposely, from which the person has no escape other than by choosing marriage.

CHAPTER 16

Canon 1673 – The following tribunals are competent in cases concerning the nullity of marriage which are not reserved to the Apostolic See:

1) the tribunal of the place where the marriage was celebrated;
2) the tribunal of the place where the respondent has a domicile or quasi-domicile;
3) the tribunal of the place where the plaintiff has a domicile, provided that both parties live within the territory of the same Episcopal Conference, and that the judicial Vicar of the domicile of the respondent, after consultation with the respondent, gives consent;
4) the tribunal of the place in which in fact most of the evidence is to be collected, provided that consent is given by the judicial Vicar of the domicile of the respondent, who must first ask the respondent whether he or she has any objection to raise.

CHAPTER 23

Canon 1142 – A non-consummated marriage between baptised persons or between a baptised party and an unbaptised party can be dissolved by the Roman Pontiff for a just reason, at the request of both parties or of either party, even if the other is unwilling.

Canon 1143,1 – In virtue of the pauline privilege, a marriage entered into by two unbaptised persons is dissolved in favour of the faith of the party who received baptism, by the very fact that a new marriage is contracted by that same party, provided the unbaptised party departs.

Canon 1143,2 The unbaptised party is considered to depart if he or she is unwilling to live with the baptised party, or to live peacefully without offence to the Creator, unless the baptised party has, after the reception of baptism, given the other just cause to depart.

Canon 18 – Laws which prescribe a penalty, or restrict the free exercise of rights, or contain an exception to the law, are to be interpreted strictly.

CHAPTER 24

Canon 213 – Christ's faithful have the right to be assisted by their Pastors from the spiritual riches of the Church, especially by the word of God and the sacraments.

Canon 912 Any baptised person who is not forbidden by law may and must be admitted to holy communion.

Canon 915 – Those upon whom the penalty of excommunication or interdict has been imposed or declared, and others who obstinately persist in manifest grave sin, are not to be admitted to holy communion.

Glossary of Terms

Advocate	One who acts to favour another's cause
Auditor	One who takes evidence on behalf of the tribunal
Bigamous marriage	A marriage entered into while still bound in a legal marriage to another
Canon law	The law of the Church
Citation	Act of calling/inviting a person to give evidence
Competence	Legal capacity of a tribunal to hear a particular case
Consent	The act by which a person commits himself or herself to marriage
Convalidate	Recognise as valid that which was legally presumed invalid
Decree of nullity	The document officially declaring that a marriage is null and void
Defender of the bond	One who acts to uphold the bond of a valid marriage
Dissolution	The breaking of a bond of marriage
Divorce	Civil dissolution of a marriage
Documentary process	Process by which nullity is proved by presentation of the appropriate documents
Equity	Justice tempered with mercy
External forum	Those areas of a person's life which are or can be generally known, e.g. marital status

Formal process	Full judicial process requiring an affirmative decision from two tribunals before a petition for nullity is granted
Instance	A case can be heard in first, second or third instance, depending on whether it is the first, second or third time that judgment has been pronounced on it
Internal forum	Matters affecting the conscience and soul and which are not public
Irregular union	A marriage which the Church does not legally recognise as valid
Legitimate	Within the law (whether valid or not)
Merely ecclesiastical law	A law which is written by the church for its own purpose and which does not find its foundation in scripture or nature
Officialis (judicial vicar)	The priest appointed by the bishop to run the tribunal in his name
Petition	The document requesting an investigation into a marriage
Petitioner/plaintiff	The party to a marriage who requests an investigation into its validity
Procurator	One who acts on behalf of another
Respondent	The (former) spouse of a petitioner
Rota	The ordinary third instance tribunal
Scandal	That which can cause another to sin (usually the sin of judging another)
Subsidiarity (principle of)	Allowing decisions to be made at the appropriate level of competent authority
Tribunal	Court established by the bishop to investigate matters of contention
Valid	All essential legal elements are in place